Transforming Insight

The 42 secrets of successful corporate Insight teams

First published in November 2020 by the Insight Management Academy,
Agriculture House, 1 Newbold Terrace, Royal Leamington Spa,
Warwickshire CV32 4EA, U.K.

ISBN 978-1-912806-01-0

For more information please contact info@insight-management.org

Design and artwork by Pip Finch, Spirit Design and Advertising

I'd like to dedicate this book to Adam Elliott, Stewart Robbins and Andy Smith, my first colleagues in the world of Insight. They taught me to ask, 'what's going on there?' and 'why is it important?'

And to Steve Wills and Sally Webb, the founders of the Insight Management Academy. They inspired me and a generation of Insight leaders to make Insight make a difference in our organisations.

Transforming Insight

Our story starts with an introduction and is then divided into five sections:

Introduction

There has never been a better time to work in a corporate Insight team. Market research and customer analysis roles have always provided intellectual challenge and the unique buzz that comes from successfully identifying a new insight about a consumer's behaviour and its effect on an organisation. However, in recent years, three major developments have had a dramatic impact on the scale of Insight teams' opportunity.

First, there has been the exponential growth in customer data, driven largely by digital transactions and social media conversations. Companies that had previously never known the identity of their end consumer now offer services online enabling them to collect vast amounts of information about customers and their relationship with our organisations.

Second, our ability to understand human behaviour has evolved significantly, in particular our comprehension of human decision-making. Developments in the fields of psychology and economics have combined to give us a rich knowledge of behavioural biases, so we now have a better idea what data to look for and a better chance of interpreting it to explain consumer choices.

And finally, a new breed of CEOs and marketing directors are preaching the importance of customer-centricity. This has led to an unprecedented increase in the demand for customer insights, and a premium paid for analysts and researchers who have the skills to ask the right questions and then manipulate and interrogate data to provide insightful answers.

Data is the world's fastest growing resource, and the appetite and ability to use customer and market data is growing exponentially. With no exaggeration, it can be said that there has never been a greater opportunity for Insight to transform the performance of an entire organisation.

Do you work for an Insight-driven organisation?

Despite this opportunity, Insight departments across every industry sector in Europe and North America regularly report that it is actually getting more difficult to do their job. The Insight Management Academy (IMA) was set up in the UK in 2004 to support corporate research and analysis teams, and it speaks to Insight leaders from multiple companies each week. And the message is consistent: the data situation may have changed, the software improved, the science developed, and the appetite increased, but how many organisations are really Insight-driven? How many companies can truly claim to have put a sophisticated, joined-up understanding of consumers right at the very centre of their decision-making processes?

How has this happened? I think that the increase in available data and ways in which it could be manipulated, together with the ever-expanding demand from decision-makers, have combined to make Insight teams more task-focused. We are doing more and more analysis and research, but in it itself this doesn't make our companies Insight-driven. Far from it.

If, as Insight leaders, we are going to seize the opportunity and really make Insight make a difference, we need to step back and reflect on the precise nature of the opportunity we have, and plan for how we are going to utilise our resources more effectively to turn opportunity into reality.

To put it another way, if we want our organisations' performance to be transformed by Insight, we first have to transform our Insight functions and the role they play in our companies.

In 2004, the IMA coined the phrase *Insight management*, defining it as the discipline of making Insight make a difference. In the sixteen years since then, the IMA has been carrying out its own research into best practice in all aspects of Insight management, providing inspiration, support and guidance to thousands of corporate Insight professionals.

This began with the creation of the Insight forum in London, a group of forty senior Insight leaders from organisations like eBay, McDonald's, Asda, Kraft-Heinz and Nestle who share a passion for seeing Insight increase its impact.

The forum has now met over sixty times in London and Manchester, with over fifty topics explored and best practice reports written. The conversation has now expanded to enable end-user Insight leaders in North America, Europe and Asia to contribute to, and benefit from, the IMA's understanding. Members range from National Public Radio of America to Carlsberg in Denmark, from Boehringer Ingelheim in Canada and Germany, to Transport for London, and Twinings in Australia.

My own career has been shaped by these ideas. In 2005 I was given a wonderful opportunity to create and lead Barclays Bank's first joined-up Insight function, comprising customer analysis, market research and competitor intelligence. Seeking inspiration, I applied for membership of the newly-formed Insight forum on behalf of the bank, and subsequently represented it at the forums for over a decade. In 2015, looking for ways I could help other Insight leaders make Insight make a difference in their companies, I joined the IMA's board of directors and have since had the luxury of spending my mornings talking to senior people in corporate Insight and my afternoons developing principles from which others could learn.

Speaking at the World Marketing Congress in Mumbai in November 2018, and shortly afterwards at the Quirk's Event in New York, I drew many of these principles together to provide an overview of the key territories that I believe all corporate Insight leaders should explore. Inspired by the reaction, I have written this book to guide anyone who believes that Insight could play a more effective role in their organisation.

Transforming Insight: the 42 secrets of successful corporate Insight teams

This book is organised into five sections:

- **Identifying value:** looks at the core purpose of an Insight team and the ways we can identify value for our organisation by generating new insights and developing customer knowledge

- **Driving change:** explores the principle that there is no point doing any research or analysis unless we then use it to drive change through communication and influence

- **Leading Insight:** challenges perceptions of the role of the Insight leader and the requirement for us to design and deliver a top-down plan for leading Insight strategy and people

- **Optimising impact:** examines the positioning of the Insight team within the organisation and the critical role played by our department's contribution to sustainable commercial success

- **Moving forwards:** suggests that the 2020 coronavirus pandemic has presented an unprecedented opportunity for Insight teams to accelerate their evolution then maintain their momentum

Each bite-sized chapter reveals one of the 42 secrets and can be read in as little as ten minutes. Whether you read the book end-to-end in a week, or use the 5-point summary on the last page of each chapter to inspire you at the start of a new day, I hope that the ideas in *Transforming Insight* become as pivotal to your career as they have been to mine.

Section 1

Identifying value for our organisations

Identifying value for our organisations

In the first section of *Transforming Insight*, we will focus on the first ten secrets of successful corporate Insight teams:

Chapter 1
What is Insight?

If you're reading this, there's a good chance that you work in an Insight team*. So what are insights?

Most people would agree that insights are not the same thing as data, or facts, or information. Insights may well be drawn from all of these, but in themselves they are not the same as insights.

Many people outside our teams might well describe Insight as market research, customer analytics or competitor intelligence. But we would say that these are labels which describe some of the functional inputs to the insight generation process. They are not the same as insights either.

So what are insights?

Confession time: before working full time with the Insight Management Academy, I ran the Insight and Analysis function at Barclays in the UK for over a decade, and during that time I didn't really put too much faith in precise definitions. I would have said that whether something was seen as insightful had as much to do with the audience and what they had previously

*NB Throughout this book I will capitalise the word Insight when referring to the concept or function, but not when it refers to discoveries or knowledge

known or not known, as it did with whether the work conformed to a specific definition. I was more interested in whether we were developing evidence-based opinions that could move the organisation in a sensible direction.

But definitions can sometimes be useful, so here goes. The IMA defines insights as:

Insights are contextualised observations about consumer value, behaviour, habits, circumstances, attitudes, market or environment that have the potential to change how an organisation acts and achieves success.

That's a lot of words, so let's focus on three parts of the definition in turn:

Insights are contextualised observations...

Insights are not isolated facts or figures, they are findings presented in the light of a wider piece of contextual understanding.

Writing this in April 2020, every day we are told how many people have been hospitalised with the coronavirus. Each instance represents a crisis for someone's family, but the daily numbers don't really mean anything as statistics in themselves. They only become insights if we are simultaneously told whether that is more hospitalisations or fewer than in previous days, more or less than our hospital capacity, more or less than expected, or the number seen in other countries.

...about consumer value, behaviour, habits, circumstances, attitudes, market or environment...

The long list in the middle – and I could have added more words to it – reflects the wide range of focus, even for a team specialising in customer and market insight. Any piece of evidence is relevant to our role if it helps us to explain how and why consumers in our market become customers of our organisation and create or destroy value for it.

It follows that there can be many types of data input to the insight generation process, including:

Customer databases: if we are lucky enough to have them, may tell us the identity of our customers, the nature of the relationship we have with them, the transactions they do, and the value of those transactions.

Internal data: other departments may supply important pieces of the knowledge jigsaw – employee interactions, operational constraints, financial implications, complaints made.

Market data: the sector in which we work will often determine our ability to analyse our own customer data versus our relative reliance on market data. But all companies need some external perspective about the volume and value in a market, their share of that market, and broader trends (consumer, demographic, societal, economic, technological, etc).

Consumer research: last but by no means least, the market research which forms the backbone of Insight work in many companies, whether it's quantitative, qualitative, ethnographic, observational research, or [insert your favourite methodology here]. We all need to talk to our customers to understand why they do what they do, and under what circumstances they might behave differently.

...that have the potential to change how an organisation acts and achieves success.

This is a key differentiator between insights and information. All progressive Insight leaders agree that insights have to be actionable, and if taken, that action would have to contribute to our organisations' success. Nine times out of ten it's possible, indeed imperative, to quantify that success with a \$ or £ sign; first to prove to ourselves that we have produced valuable insights, and second in order to demonstrate the benefit of our recommendations to decision-makers.

So that's the IMA's definition of insights. Feel free to produce your own if you prefer different words. But check that your definition covers the same bases, otherwise there's a risk that your Insight team will go on to define its work too narrowly.

What is insight?

We now have an answer to the question, 'what are insights?' but does that mean that we also know the answer to a second question, 'what is insight?'

Not necessarily.

If insights are individual, contextualised discoveries, insight is the accumulated understanding that is built up from many insights. It relates to the process of collating evidence and findings from multiple projects and sources, reflecting on the connections, and investigating the contradictions.

It's this bigger picture that enables corporate Insight professionals to form evidence-based opinions that explain to themselves and others how and why consumers in our market become customers of our organisation, and how they create or destroy value for it.

The starting point for anyone wanting their Insight function to make a difference in their organisation is to understand the definition of insights and insight and the difference between them.

....

The 1st secret of successful Insight teams is that they agree a progressive definition of insights and insight as a basis for all their subsequent activity

If you would like to explore this topic further, you might like to read the IMA's Insight leader guide *IMP101: An introduction to Insight generation*

....

Key points to consider:

1. Insights are contextualised observations, not data, or isolated facts and figures

2. Insights can relate to anything that helps explain why consumers in a market become customers of an organisation, and create value for it

3. Insights can be drawn from a wide range of internal and external data sources

4. Insights must have the potential to change how an organisation acts and achieves success

5. Insight is the collective knowledge that comes from many insights plus our understanding about the connections between them

So that's insights and insight. What are the implications for the work of Insight teams? That's the question we'll explore in the next chapter.

Chapter 2
What's the purpose of Insight?

In the first chapter we defined insights and insight. Presumably it follows that an Insight team (as they are usually called in the UK, or Insights team in the US) spends its time producing a combination of insights and insight?

I think the best answer to that is: sometimes. Let me explain...

The IMA carries out a lot of capability benchmarking to help organisations in the UK, North America and Europe to better understand their Insight capability. The fact that Insight leaders have approached us in the first place is usually a sign that they have thought about the role of their Insight team in its organisation, but they also recognise that they still have much to learn from other Insight leaders.

What are the most common findings? Well unfortunately, despite best intentions, many Insight leaders when asked about their teams, will recognise that they:

- Spend more time producing data, facts and figures than real insights

- Find it difficult to devote much time at all to joining the dots between projects

- React as a service function to research and data requests from other departments

- Lose sight of what happens once decision-makers have received their reports

- Are so busy peddling on the corporate hamster wheel that they don't reflect on the underlying purpose of Insight

Insight is an expensive business. It costs a lot of money to acquire data, to manage it, to analyse it, to buy market research from agencies, to employ people with analytical or research skills. It takes a lot of time and effort to recruit Insight teams, to manage them, to supervise their work and support them as individuals.

So, like every corporate department, we have a collective responsibility to make sure that our organisations are getting the best possible return on their investment, otherwise there's a good chance that those resources would be better deployed elsewhere.

If our organisations are going to get the most value from Insight, those of us responsible for our Insight teams need to transform them from service functions to proactive business drivers. When other departments ask us to jump, we should stop asking 'how high?' and instead ask about the business decisions they are hoping to make. Then reflect on the broad range of ways we could inform those decisions.

We should also study our own organisations with the same focus we bring to studying our customers and our market. Why? Because insights have no value unless they are actioned, and whether they are actioned depends in practice not just on the quality of those insights but on how we share our learning with those making big decisions. Sometimes we know exactly who these people are, and we can try to build personal relationships with them. But often key decisions will be taken when we are not in the room and we will only find out about it after the fact; therefore, we need to broaden everyone's understanding to safeguard busy executives from making Insight-free decisions.

The most effective Insight teams therefore concentrate their efforts on four activities:

Insight generation: they investigate business issues and produce real insights – those contextualised observations about consumer value, behaviour, habits, circumstances, attitudes, market or environment that have the potential to change how an organisation acts and achieves success.

Insight knowledge: they recognise that there is always going to be more value in accumulated knowledge and understanding than in a single new piece of research or analysis; so they manage their time and resources so that they can develop joined-up, big picture insight about consumers in a market becoming customers of an organisation, and creating or destroying value for it.

Insight influence: they identify the most important decisions that a company needs to make, and develop relationships with the executives who will make them, also recognising that in a high-pressure environment the most enlightened decision-makers will sometimes need a little nudge to adopt the best course.

Insight communication: they see it as their mission to share key customer and market insights across the organisation so that these insights are present in every room where key decisions are being taken, even if the Insight team itself was unaware that the meeting was taking place.

Tasks and purpose

Having benchmarked over 200 organisations in the UK, North America and Europe in the last couple of years, we can say with confidence that there is no Insight team in the world that is as good as it could be on all four of those tasks. But there is a marked difference in effectiveness between those that recognise that it's their responsibility to focus on all four and those that don't.

But the most effective Insight teams share another attribute. They don't just work at the task-level, they reflect on their underlying purpose and use this insight about themselves as a reference point and source of inspiration. We will look at the topics of Insight strategy, ambition, vision and positioning later in this book, but I need to put a stake in the ground at this point.

Too many Insight teams define their role too narrowly, often because they start with the data they habitually analyse, or the research methodologies in which they have most expertise. The most effective Insight teams see good data, great research, and critical thinking as means to an end, not the end itself.

The most progressive Insight teams recognise that they have an underlying purpose, which is to identify value for their organisation and to drive change within it.

....

The 2nd secret of successful Insight teams is that they recognise an underlying purpose: to identify value and drive change

If you would like to explore this topic further, you might like to read the IMA's Insight leader guide *IMP101: An introduction to Insight generation*

....

Key points to consider:

1. Insight teams should generate new insights about big business issues, not respond to requests for data and market research

2. We should cultivate and harvest accumulated knowledge about consumers in our market and customers of our organisation

3. We need to influence senior decision-makers on specific issues based on both new insights and accumulated insight

4. We also have to communicate insight across our organisation so that all key decision-makers know fundamental customer truths

5. The underlying purpose of Insight is to identify value for our organisations and drive change within them

Now that we have defined insights, insight, and the underlying purpose of an Insight team, what is the implication for the way that our departments should look at business issues? That's the question we'll explore in the next chapter.

Chapter 3
From the market to the money

If our organisations are to succeed, they need joined-up insights. They don't need isolated facts and figures, they need contextualised observations, new discoveries about how customers think and behave in the market in which we operate. If these discoveries are to have any interest, validity, sense of proportion or importance, they have to be generated in the context of other known truths. Business success relies on joined-up insights.

In 2004 the IMA published the report that first coined the phrase *Insight management*. It recommended that organisations should first nail the real issue or opportunity to be investigated, and then take a joined-up approach to solving that issue. What had been separate functions like market research, competitor intelligence and customer analysis would be far more effective if they worked together. The individual disciplines were important to produce robust, accurate inputs, but the ultimate outputs should be joined-up insights to enable our companies to take joined-up decisions.

Does your company create joined-up insights?

But 15 years later, how many organisations consistently produce joined-up insights? In its daily conversations with corporate Insight leaders in the UK, North America and Europe, the IMA usually hears one of three stories:

- Market research and analytics are sitting in different business silos with corporate decision-makers forced to choose which department they go to

- Market research and analytics are in the same business unit, but are working on separate sets of projects, with different mindsets, approaches, and contexts for their work

- Market research leaders are taking on some responsibility for analysts or, even more common, analytics departments are taking over market research teams, but neither knows how to get the best out of the other

In each case, the generation of new insights, and the input to corporate decision-making, usually remains fragmented. So how can we Insight leaders change our thinking – and our colleagues' working patterns – to create the joined-up insights necessary for better business decisions?

How to create joined-up insights

The answer is to reframe our approach to Insight activity. We should move away from a focus on functional disciplines like market research, customer analytics and competitor intelligence, and instead see each as inputs to the creation of a holistic story about how consumers in our market become customers of our organisation and create value for it.

To do this consistently, we should adopt a causal model into which we can add every new piece of knowledge. The IMA calls this the *MADE in Insight* model:

Metrics: the business outcomes our organisation aspires to achieve. If the purpose of Insight is to drive better decisions and improve our company's performance, then it's no surprise that a major requirement of all Insight projects is that they include a focus on the metrics we are trying to move in our organisation.

The IMA embeds this focus in its overall approach to generating new insights, recognising that the place that most projects go wrong is right at the very start when too many researchers and analysts react to a request for information without taking the time to nail the underlying business issue. However, a focus on business outcomes doesn't stop when we have nailed the underlying problem at the start of the project. At every step of the subsequent investigation we need to use those business metrics as a key reference point.

The best pieces of Insight focus on financial outcomes and use commercial language to describe their observations and recommendations. So you might want to think of Metrics as Money.

Activity: the customer behaviour that directly affects those business outcomes. One step along the line from Metrics, is Activity, in other words the customer behaviour that has, or could have, a direct impact on our key business outcomes. We are starting to move into territory that more Insight teams like to explore, because it looks outward to our customers rather than inward to our business performance.

Just as with Metrics, it is perfectly possible to carry out interesting analysis on data that relates purely to Activity. But the critical thing is to focus on understanding customer behaviour that links directly to business outcomes.

Decisions: the consumer choices that really drive customer behaviour. We have now moved to the third part of our MADE in Insight model. The Decision category is at the very heart of traditional Insight work, and the focus for most market researchers in particular. It encompasses questions such as why do customers shop with us, how would consumers in our market respond if we launched a new product, and what underlying need or aspiration really drives consumer behaviour?

Environment: the market context that frames those choices. The final category of the *MADE in Insight* model is Environment. This is not just a focus on green issues – although they will certainly be one aspect to consider in many sectors. It's the whole environment in which consumers live and make choices, and the trends that take place, sometimes quickly, sometimes so slowly they are almost imperceptible.

Environment is not about individuals, it's about the whole market and the factors that shape the decisions of segments, generations or populations.

Insight teams tend to focus too narrowly on one type of data or methodology, drilling into detail on customer Activity, for example, or the consumer Decisions associated with a particular issue. Too often we do not take the full breadth of the issue into account.

Insight projects that do not consider Decisions and Environment are not anchored in the real world in which consumers live. However, we will not identify value or drive change if our findings and recommendations do not revolve around customer Activity and those financial outcome Metrics.

MADE or EDAM... Where should we start? We can actually start at either end, depending on the nature of the business issue we are looking at. Analytical investigations into trading performance, for example, will start with the Metrics; whereas New Product Development research might well start with the Environment. But the key thing is that in all projects we must map from the market to the money.

....

The 3rd secret of successful Insight teams is that they map every business issue from the market to the money

If you would like to explore this topic further, you might like to read the IMA's Insight leader guide *IMP102: How to create joined-up Insight*

....

Key points to consider:

1. Business success requires joined-up insights, so we need to take each issue and map from the market to the money
2. Metrics: the business outcomes, usually related to money, that our organisation aspires to achieve
3. Activity: the customer behaviour that directly affects those business outcomes
4. Decisions: the consumer choices that really drive that behaviour
5. Environment: the market context that frames those choices

But what happens if we don't know all the numbers we would like to know about all the aspects captured in the MADE in Insight model? Don't panic! It's almost inevitable that we won't be able to find every number we need but there are ways of dealing with it, as we'll see in the next chapter.

Chapter 4
Making up the numbers

Does your Insight team make up its numbers? The very idea probably fills you with horror. But I'm going to argue that making up the numbers is actually a critical skill for everyone in Insight.

I said in the introduction that it's a great time to be in Insight. And it is! Almost without exception, our organisations at least claim to recognise the need for a more data-led, Insight-driven approach to decision-making. The demand for greater knowledge about customers, the decisions they make, and the drivers of those decisions, is ever increasing.

It follows that many organisations are now investing more in their analytics capability, whether its in data and software, or in the people with the right skillsets. At the IMA we believe this represents a huge opportunity for the role that Insight can play in driving our organisations. In the best cases, Insight professionals are now seen as the translators within our businesses, making the links from the data and research to the key decisions.

However, to support agile decision-making, our senior stakeholders often need answers fast, even if it's just 'something to work with'. So, for every decision, a trade-off needs to be made between perfect insights and agile decisions. This middle ground is where the most workable solutions are found.

Agile decision-making vs good quality insights

The IMA's Julia Joskey believes that there are four key aspects that every Insight team should explore to bridge the gap between agile decision-making and good quality insights. These are:

- Understand the difference between accuracy and precision
- Use BOEING to scope issues with rough calculations
- Find big numbers to put other numbers into content
- Practice your mental maths and use shortcuts to make sums easier

We'll look at each of these in turn.

First, it's really important that anyone working in Insight understands the difference between precision and accuracy. Does your Insight team focus on generating precise data or accurate insights? A measurement that is accurate but not precise can still be helpful. But a measurement that is precise but inaccurate is not just unhelpful, it's often dangerously misleading. It's better to be broadly right than precisely wrong.

As a society we tend to put a lot of faith in precision. We have seen lots of examples of this during the coronavirus crisis where statistics such as the number of people tested, infected or hospitalised have been quoted in very precise terms. And precision is often valued above everything in our companies as well, and rightly so in departments like Finance, Operations and HR.

But some customer and market issues do not lend themselves to precision. This is partly because of the issues themselves – how consumers feel, for example, why they act in a particular way, the likely size of a market for a new product before it's launched. It can also be due to the partial or imperfect data available to us to solve problems. In many instances, an accurate range of outcomes is far more useful in Insight than a precise number that will almost certainly never be right and might well give a false impression of confidence.

The second point is to adopt a back of an envelope approach when we first start thinking about a problem or a question. Before we do any analysis or research, it's helpful to do some rough calculations to understand the size and scope of what we're dealing with. The IMA's co-founder, Steve Wills, calls this the BOEING technique: Back Of an Envelope INtelligent Guesswork.

For example, if you were doing some work on the new automobile market in Canada, and you didn't know how big it was, you could probably make a reasonable estimate using BOEING. If you knew how many adults lived in Canada, you could then estimate the number who drive, and the proportion of the drivers who own their vehicle, and in turn what percentage might buy a new car each year. None of these estimates would be exactly right but combining them in a logical sequence would help you to identify a sense of the scale. You can then talk to others or do some digging to refine your estimate.

BOEING relies on a combination of facts, assumptions and logic. Facts should be the things we can all agree on, likewise the logic of how you put the elements in any calculation together to produce an overall estimate. But the critical element is often the assumptions we use to fill the gaps. This bit might surprise you, but we actually want our stakeholders to challenge our assumptions when we use BOEING. This is because our stakeholders may be in a better position to supply an accurate figure, but also because being transparent about our assumptions helps us to work collaboratively with others and get to better answers.

The third aspect is to know how to handle big numbers. Insight is so often all about perspective: if we can understand the context, the bigger picture, we can find the best ways to interpret a new number or finding without getting lost in the detail.

This is such an important aspect of Insight work. Every day we face situations in our organisations when we see people react to numbers without having an appropriate perspective and sense of scale. I think this is particularly the case for customer and market data, because Insight teams tend to be the only functions within many companies that look at these. By contrast, sales figures, revenue, number of employees, etc, are often numbers that many people in the company know well, in fact they may even be in the public domain. So, let it be our mission to never report a new finding without first providing the context; never supply a new number without first giving our audience an existing number that will help them to evaluate the new one.

The final point is about improving our mental maths. People commonly make mistakes in mental arithmetic. It's pretty easy to get a decimal point in the wrong place or miss a zero off somewhere. But the good news for all of us is that it gets easier the more you practice, especially if we focus on getting to a reasonably accurate answer, not a really precise one.

One technique for making our mental maths easier is explained by Rob Eastaway in his great book, *Maths on the Back of an Envelope*. Rob advocates the 'Zequals method' – a technique where you round every number you see to one significant figure (so 365 becomes 400, and 5,326 million becomes 5 billion). This massively reduces the complexity of any sum we want to do in our heads and is a great shortcut both for our BOEINGs and for appreciating the relative size of big numbers.

Adopting these four practices can help us to develop better perspective, enhance our agility, and give us greater confidence and credibility with decision-makers. So if your Insight team doesn't 'make up the numbers' yet, now's the time to start.

....

The 4th secret of successful Insight teams is that they value accuracy over precision and take a creative approach to estimating numbers

If you would like to explore this topic further, you might like to read the IMA's Insight leader guide *IMP103: How to make up the numbers*

....

Key points to consider:

1. To be effective, Insight professionals need to balance the drive for perfect insights with the need to support agile decision-making
2. Understand the difference between accuracy and precision: in Insight it's better to be broadly right than precisely wrong
3. At the start of any research or analysis, use the BOEING technique to do some rough calculations on the size and scope of the issue
4. To effectively handle big numbers, first strive to identify some even bigger numbers that provide the context and true sense of scale
5. Practice your mental maths skills, and find useful shortcuts to make your sums easier

So far we've looked at how to map our business issues, and how to deal with gaps in our knowledge. But what steps should we follow when decision-makers ask us to work on a new piece of research or analysis? That's the topic we'll look at in the next chapter.

Chapter 5
Nailing the real issue

No Insight team can be effective without developing the ability to routinely discover new insights. But if you attend a market research conference or listen to an agency proposal you could easily think that the process of generating insights is shrouded in mystery. Some people use the analogy of alchemy, the science of turning base metals into gold. Others describe generating insights as a quest for the Holy Grail.

The IMA believes that it really doesn't have to be this complicated. It should be perfectly possible for intelligent people to draw commercially useful conclusions and recommendations from data and observations without the need for magic spells.

So are we good at producing new insights?

Many Insight teams are not producing as many good insights as they should be. Insight leaders around the world routinely describe how their teams' time is spent answering data questions, or managing research projects, the brief for which has been handed to them by other departments in the business.

The wider organisation's appetite for more facts and figures can then encourage management to recruit more fact-finders, so the department that is supposed to be responsible for advising the company on how to be more successful using customer and market knowledge ends up being a data factory.

How can we generate better insights?

In the last two chapters we have looked at the importance of mapping business issues from the market to the money and striking a balance between perfect data and agile insight. But what do we actually do when faced with a stakeholder who wants some support? We should:

1. First nail the underlying business issue that we need to address

2. Adopt detective skills to run a joined-up Insight investigation

It's the second of these that usually gets most attention: the detective bit, the gathering of data and the process of deduction that leads to the 'aha!' moments. But Einstein said that if he had an hour to solve a problem, he would spend fifty-five minutes thinking about the underlying problem and five minutes thinking about the solution to it, so in this chapter we're going to consider the 'nailing' and in the next chapter we'll look at the 'investigating'.

How can we nail the business issue?

Most Insight projects fail because they start in the wrong place. Our analysts and researchers take a request for information – information that somebody else believes to be relevant to one part of an issue - and dutifully conduct research or analysis to find that data. If our teams want to generate real insights that solve business issues, we have to move away from taking data requests and research briefs. We have to change our mindset and improve our ability to nail the underlying business issue that needs to be solved.

The IMA recommends a 3-step RED process:

Reflect: before we respond to requests from stakeholders, let's stop and think. What's the context for the question being asked? What do we know about this market, customer segment, brand or product from previous analysis? What do we know about the revenue and costs associated with it? What has our company tried to do before in this space? What is it trying to do now?

Engage: we cannot generate insights in a vacuum, we need to speak to business decision-makers. The stakeholder who asked us for the new research might have a clever plan for how they are going to use the new data to help them to solve a problem or seize a new opportunity. Or they might be passing along a request from their boss, which has probably gone to other departments as well, sowing the seed for contradictory data and a confused strategy. You decide which is more likely in your company!

But every member of the IMA has found that they can generate better insights by talking to decision-makers, probing their assumptions, providing context and challenge to the way a problem has been framed.

Diagnose: the underlying issue, just like a doctor or a management consultant. The IMA's co-founder, Sally Webb, introduced the SCQAB model for structuring Insight projects, based on Barbara Minto's SCQA model for training management consultants. Let's consider this tool in more detail.

Adopting the consultant's approach

SCQAB stands for situation, complication, question, answer and benefit:

Situation describes the background to the Insight investigation. It involves capturing key stats about customer segments or the wider market which forces the analyst or researcher to recognise the big picture context.

Complication captures the aspects that have changed or challenged assumptions. These are often the reason why the business is now asking for some insights, and in a commercial world there is a good chance that the prompt has been some adverse financial numbers.

Question is the real business question that we arrive at having established the Situation and the Complication. In this section we capture, in as few words as possible, the real underlying business issue that needs to be addressed. As we have seen above, this will often be different to the question that the Insight team initially received. Once captured, this key Question will frame the rest of the project, during which we'll complete our Answer and Benefit sections.

So, I'm with Einstein on this one: it is worth investing proper time getting the question right. In a commercial organisation, the key question should relate to profit in some way and be stated in financial terms. Not only is this an important check that you have really got to the nub of the issue, it will also be a lot easier to sell in your recommendations for action at the end if everything comes with a $ sign.

....

The 5th secret of successful Insight teams is that they nail the underlying business issue before they begin any new research or analysis

If you would like to explore this topic further, you might like to read the IMA's Insight leader guide *IMP104: How to nail the business issue*

....

Key points to consider:

1. Before we can begin the detective work, we can nail the underlying business issue to be solved using the RED model
2. Reflect on the context that sits behind requests for research and analysis and what relevant insights have been captured before
3. Engage with senior decision-makers, asking questions about their assumptions
4. Diagnose the underlying business issue using SCQAB
5. The SCQ frames the rest of the Insight project, the A and B will be completed as we solve the problem

The Answer and Benefit sections of the model cannot be completed until the investigation is further advanced. But it is good to begin with the end in mind and remember throughout any subsequent investigation that we need to address that key question. How we go about doing it will be the topic for our next chapter.

Chapter 6
Insight investigations

In the last chapter we looked at the importance of nailing the issue before launching new pieces of analysis or research. What happens next will depend on the question you have identified and the sources of information and data collection available to you.

However, effective Insight teams tend to adopt a common mindset regardless of whether they are data analysts, quantitative, qualitative or desk researchers. It's the mindset of the detective.

There are four broad stages involved in every Insight investigation, but the sequence can vary because of the iterative nature of good Insight work.

Stage 1: Generate hypotheses

Having nailed the business issue, most good analysts and researchers will then spend some time generating hypotheses. These are educated guesses about what the answer to the underlying business question might be. What could be the best way to increase sales, or reduce customer attrition? How might we best spend our advertising budget or improve customer satisfaction?

Whole books could be written about how to generate hypotheses, but in the IMA's experience they tend to come from a blend of previous experience, existing insights, and talking to others with relevant business knowledge.

Really good analysts and researchers are likely to be proven problem-solvers, so they probably generate hypotheses without even thinking about it.

Just as we saw with nailing the issue, management consultants tend to be very good at envisioning possible solutions at an early stage of new projects. This is partly because of their experience, and the skillset that they have developed, but also because they tend to use tools like decision trees and mindmaps that can help us all to spot areas to investigate.

But you might be thinking at this point, 'wait, surely we can't start thinking of possible answers before we've even got into our investigation?' In fact it's really important that we do, because insights very rarely emerge from random trawls through unconnected data. The IMA's Jane Woolley, a former Head of Insight at London Underground, describes this phenomenon as being 'more like Columbo than Columbus'. We may set sail to explore the wide ocean and strike lucky by stumbling upon America; but we're far more likely to have repeated success by identifying good lines of enquiry right at the start of our investigation. Just like every TV detective.

There is, of course, a danger of confirmation bias: that we find evidence that neatly fits our starting hypothesis and ignores data which doesn't support it. That's clearly wrong, and unprofessional; we need to spend as long trying to disprove our hypotheses as to validate them. But we are still better off starting with hypotheses and adapting them to the data as we go along than starting with a blank sheet of paper and hoping for a Eureka! moment.

Stage 2: Explore the evidence

For many people in Insight this is the fun bit. Finding new database variables, hearing views expressed in a focus group, identifying fresh perspectives using a new research technique. Good Insight professionals have to display curiosity about customers, markets and their own business. The urge to find out new things, identify patterns that nobody else has seen, make a connection that suddenly makes sense of customer behaviour... these are a few of our favourite things.

In chapter 3 we looked at the importance of mapping from the market to the money and suggested that the *MADE in Insight* model (Metrics, Activity, Decisions, Environment) provided a good template for mapping our business issues. It can also be useful as we explore them as it helps to offset our natural tendency to select the data or the technique with which we are most comfortable at the expense of using a wide variety of sources to produce comprehensive recommendations. There is a classic trade-off between wanting to drill into more and more detail and remembering that Insight projects have to address the overall business issue.

Stage 3: Interpreting the evidence

Consultants sometimes talk about 'diamond-shaped' thinking: you start with a simple view of an issue, then your comprehension of the different aspects grows as you investigate it; but you have to reach a point where you turn a corner and focus on a manageable number of aspects that are going to form the basis of your recommendations. In reality this process doesn't just happen once in the course of a project, it happens multiple times at different levels. We are constantly casting our net, hauling in the fish, discarding the ones we don't want, then starting again.

The exploration phase of Insight work is akin to the top half of the diamond – the more we explore, the more we discover. The interpretation phase is where we turn the corner: we sift the evidence, we decide what's important and what isn't, and how the important pieces of evidence can be stitched together in a constantly evolving story. This is one part of our Insight investigation where two heads are better than one: use one of your colleagues as a sounding board, get them to challenge your interpretation, or help you to make sense of inconsistent findings.

Stage 4: Form an opinion

This final stage is an uncomfortable one for some people. We probably all know analysts who would rather present us with data and leave us to form a view of the 'so what' and 'now what'. If you have some of these people in your team, a good development step can be to ask them to identify and evaluate a small range of options. This can feel safer than having to come down on one side of the fence about what should happen next. It can also be a canny way of persuading others to buy into your findings.

Conversely, there are some naturally opinionated analysts and researchers who are always keen to share their views. But we must make sure that these views address that underlying business issue that we identified in our SCQAB.

....

The 6th secret of successful Insight teams is that they take a detective approach to Insight investigations

If you would like to explore this topic further, you might like to read the IMA's Insight leader guide *IMP105: How to approach Insight investigations*

....

Key points to consider:

1. Effective Insight teams recruit and develop detectives with a natural curiosity about customers, markets and their own business

2. Insight investigations should start with hypotheses about the likely answers, but we should try to validate these and disprove them

3. The exploration phase of Insight investigations is likely to involve multiple data sources and techniques

4. Insight detectives need to interpret the evidence they discover, asking 'what?', 'so what?' and 'now what?'

5. The objective of Insight investigations is to develop options and provide an evidence-based opinion about what our businesses should do

We should also remember that each Insight project is itself part of a wider process of knowledge creation, and we also need to form big picture opinions about customers, markets and our business options. It's that topic of knowledge development that we'll discuss in the next chapter.

Chapter 7
The evolution to Insight farming

At the start of this book we looked at the definition of insights and insight, and the purpose of an Insight team. We have then focused on the insights bit – the discovery of new, contextualised findings that have the potential to transform how our organisations do business.

No Insight team can be effective without the ability to routinely discover new insights. But is that enough?

In 2005 I was given the opportunity to lead Barclays first combined Insight team, incorporating market research, market analysis, customer analysis and competitor intelligence for its UK Retail Bank. Keen to improve the department's visibility and impact, I worked hard to get into senior executives' diaries and talk to them about our projects. At that time Barclays was recruiting a lot of new senior managers from the USA, and after a while I found myself invited to their induction meetings, marched into the room as part of these new executives' introduction to the bank.

But what I discovered was that the more senior the audience, the less they wanted to know about Insight *projects*. They didn't really want to know about the findings from particular pieces of analysis or research. What interested them was the big picture understanding that we had developed off the back of hundreds of different projects. They wanted to know how and why consumers in our market became customers of our organisation, and how they created or destroyed value for it.

The problem for me then, and I think the problem for many Insight leaders today, is that whilst we will have an instinctive understanding of part of this picture, it's a bit hit and miss, for two reasons. First, Insight projects tend to be planned bottom-up: we look back on our work each year and see a collection of projects undertaken to support different decisions, not one comprehensive piece of work to which the individual pieces of research and analysis have contributed. Second, the vast majority of our Insight specialists' time is spent working on new projects, so when senior people ask us to explain the big picture, we often have to think on our feet, and there's every chance that our colleagues would come up with a different answer.

If Insight teams are responsible for *insight* as well as *insights*, we need to transform the way we plan our time, allocate resources and measure success. We need to move away from a world where we spend all our days hunting for new insights and recognise that wise Insight teams know that Insight *farming* is more valuable to their organisations and more sustainable for the team itself.

Do you hunt insights, or farm insight?

It's worth exploring the farming analogy, because it helps explain something fundamental about the evolution of Insight teams and what sets the most effective teams apart.

- Farmers balance the short-term need to make an income, with the long-term stewardship of their land

- Farmers value experience and use it to develop a big picture view of how all the elements of nature combine to shape their environment

- Farmers prepare the ground carefully, tilling the soil and sowing their seeds

- Farmers have the patience to cultivate their crops, investing in irrigation systems that will sustain the land for many years

- Farmers can harvest from their fields time and again, and they have the satisfaction of knowing that they are feeding the nation, not just hunting for their own pleasure

What has all this got to do with Insight teams? I think that too often Insight teams act like hunters: we get drawn into the thrill of the chase as we hunt down new findings; then, having hit our target, we move onto the next one. I'm not saying that we don't need to run new Insight investigations, but putting all our focus into new projects means that we never have time to reflect on all the things that we already know, make connections we hadn't spotted, investigate contradictions, and come up with a comprehensive view of our customers, our markets, and our organisations.

The IMA would argue that there is always going to be more value in accumulated knowledge than in a single new project. Therefore, it stands to reason that our companies can make a better return on their Insight investment if we devote a significant part of our resources to farming our existing findings, and seeing each new project as one more piece of a far bigger jigsaw puzzle.

Driven by a desire to re-align what Barclays senior executives needed and what our Insight team was working on, I focused a lot of my energy for the next ten years on re-balancing our focus on new research and analysis with the broader imperative to develop a knowledge asset for our organisation. And we discovered that the apparent contradiction between the two activities was often quite superficial, and time invested in managing the collective customer and market knowledge base paid back many times over.

You would be forgiven for thinking that time spent ploughing through previous projects rather than quickly moving onto the next one is unlikely to pay back very quickly. But what you find is that developing this big picture knowledge means that you can both cut out duplication and respond in a far more agile way when someone next asks you a question. You can also offer decision-makers a choice: take a broad understanding based on previous work straight away; or spend money and wait several weeks for the results of new research.

You can also produce better insights every day, because, if insights are contextualised observations, it's your customer and market knowledge base that provides a lot of the context that we need to interpret the new things we see. It's the knowledge base that provides perspective and those really big numbers that give us a sense of scale when looking at new numbers.

....

The 7th secret of successful Insight teams is that they aspire to be Insight farmers, cultivating and harvesting accumulated knowledge

If you would like to explore this topic further, you might like to read the IMA's Insight leader guide *IMP201: An introduction to farming Insight knowledge*

....

Key points to consider:

1. Progressive Insight teams recognise their responsibility to produce big picture *insight* as well as new *insights*

2. This takes a different mindset, more akin to Insight farming than hunting

3. Insight farming takes time and patience to plough through previous research and cultivate knowledge

4. But Insight teams can reap the reward as they cut out duplication and produce better, more contextualised insights

5. Insight farming is ultimately more worthwhile, more sustainable, and supports more agile decision-making

The evolution from hunter-gathering to farming the land was a critical step for human society. The drive to become Insight farmers is just as critical for researchers and analysts who want their department to have a sustainable impact in their organisation. What's the first step in the process? That's what we'll look at in the next chapter.

Chapter 8
Sowing the seeds

It is very rare to find a progressive Insight leader who doesn't believe that there isn't more latent value in accumulated knowledge than in the next research or analysis project. Insight farming appeals to many on a cultural level, as well as offering obvious cost savings by cutting out project duplication. Good researchers and analysts are constantly accumulating knowledge in their heads anyway, so Insight farming is a logical extension for the collective Insight team.

However, very few Insight leaders think that they have yet managed to strike the right balance between running new projects and developing their knowledge base. The IMA has benchmarked over 200 organisations in the last three years, and the scores for Insight knowledge rank seventh out of the eight territories we explore. So what are the practical steps to take if you want to make Insight farming a reality?

We are going to look at three:

1. Sowing the seeds: crystallising and recording new findings
2. Cultivating knowledge: actively managing and discussing what you know
3. Farming systems: investing in systems to facilitate each part of the process and help you to harvest better insight

Crystallising and recording insights

The starting point is to recognise that we need to sow our own seeds if we hope to cultivate useful knowledge for our companies. This is where we need to look at our raw material – insights from previous projects.

If your Insight team uses the SCQAB model to focus your investigation on tight business questions this will naturally force you to distil your findings into opinions and recommendations, and you will already have many seeds ready to sow. But if some of your team's output takes the form of data tables, or old-fashioned market research debriefs that run to fifty slides or more, then there's going to be some preparatory work to do to distil existing findings into useful insights.

It's also important to remember that great ideas don't just come from formal projects. Analysts talking about an issue across the desk can come up with a really useful view that can fertilise other thinking. But we need to capture these ideas, which usually means getting them down on paper before we move onto something else. When I ran an Insight team and I overheard my colleagues discussing new ideas, I always experienced a momentary anxiety that the idea would get lost unless someone recorded it. Once it was in a document, ideally a 1-page summary with perhaps a chart, a heading that summarised the idea, and very brief supporting bullet points, then I could relax knowing that we wouldn't lose it.

'Fundamental truths' are another critical input to the Insight farming process. For example, in financial services, life-stage and life events dictate most consumer needs; and in the UK, customers sometimes seem to be born with an attitude to the big banks because family associations with them are so strong. Insights like this don't come from specific pieces of work, but they are ever-present factors, the like of which exist for all markets and contextualise all new findings. The Insight farming process will uncover far more of these over time, but it's important to capture those that already exist in individuals' heads.

Who should do this work? Who should spend time – and it does take time – to identify and file the explicit outputs from previous work as well as those implicit fundamental truths? In a perfect world I would like to believe that everyone in an Insight team should take part; the distillation, crystallisation and recording forming an integral part of each project. However, there are two problems with this: time and talent.

In any good Insight team there will inevitably be pressure to support the rest of the business on the next decisions it needs to take, and the best analysts and researchers will be in heavy demand. Personally, I would always insist that the individual leading on a project documented the key findings from it, which might involve the creation of a separate 1-page summary in addition to the report sent to the business decision-maker. But the demand for these specialists to start the next piece of research, and indeed their proximity to the detail, might not make them the best person to go back through the project and pick out all the findings you want to store for future use.

The other issue is skillset. Great data analysts and quantitative market researchers in particular need to have an eye for detail. Accurate data collection and manipulation needs a degree of precision – providing that doesn't get in the way of accuracy as we saw in chapter 4. But reviewing projects, sifting through evidence from multiple pieces of analysis to find those critical seeds which will contribute in time to your Insight harvest, that's a different skillset. It requires big picture awareness, lateral thinking, an ability to step back from the detail and identify patterns across multiple projects.

From 2005, Barclays and a range of other leading companies introduced *Insight manager* roles. The label has become quite common over the last fifteen years, and sometimes, unfortunately, it is just a label given to traditional analyst or research roles. But in the best cases, Insight managers are recruited and developed in recognition of the importance of Insight farming. We will see some of the other responsibilities they can have a little later in this book, but the first requirement is that they make sure that everything unearthed in day to day research is sifted for interest and potential future value.

....

The 8th secret of successful Insight teams is that they sow the seeds of Insight knowledge by crystallising and recording their findings

If you would like to explore this topic further, you might like to read the IMA's Insight leader guide *IMP202: How to sow the seeds of Insight knowledge*

....

Key points to consider:

1. Many Insight leaders like the idea of becoming Insight farmers, but to make it a reality takes time and focus
2. We cannot harvest knowledge without first sowing our own seeds, sifting through each project for key findings and interesting ideas
3. We should also add the implicit understanding that experienced researchers and analysts have developed over many years
4. Insight farming requires everyone to realise that no project is complete until its findings have been distilled and recorded
5. Some progressive Insight teams have introduced Insight managers to identify interesting nuggets and broader patterns

Several times in this chapter I've mentioned the need to document findings and file them, which begs two questions: how do we organise our filing, and on what systems does it take place? These are the questions that we'll consider in the next, and final, two chapters of this section.

Chapter 9
Cultivating knowledge

Sowing the seeds is the first stage in Insight farming, giving us the inputs to the overall process. As we sift through our projects we may find an immediate payback in the form of golden nuggets that are of interest to senior decision-makers. But if we want to produce a crop that we can harvest year after year, in other words a knowledge base that underpins all our future research and supports multiple business decisions, then we need to cultivate our insight. This requires more time and effort.

The idea that we should actively manage our knowledge base can seem like a really nebulous concept, so I'm going to describe a way of tackling it in very basic terms.

Stage 1 may be as simple as listing the key findings from all the best pieces of work your Insight team has done in the last year. If you have a 1-page summary, or a killer slide, for each of these pieces, you can simply stitch them together to form a 'greatest hits' compilation. That in itself would give you something to talk about when a new CEO or CMO joined the business. It can also provide a playlist for everyone in the Insight team, so that rather than defaulting to talking about just the projects they have individually worked on, there's a collective sense of Insight's most important findings.

Stage 2 might be to take a step back and consider the most significant pieces done over several years, to avoid the random effect of which decisions you have been asked to support over a short period of time. If you work in a company where consumer research, market analysis, customer analytics and competitor intelligence happen in a range of business divisions, this is also a good opportunity for each of the Insight teams to compile their own list. An early, but important stage for the evolution of Insight in my previous company was a presentation that brought together the top ten insights from analysis, with the top ten market research findings, and the top ten from competitor intelligence. Because our analysis tended to relate to customer behaviour, and our research to customer needs and the drivers of behaviour, this approach naturally started to group the types of things we had discovered.

Stage 3 starts to get to the heart of knowledge cultivation. The focus here is to group work not by when it was done, or by which branch of Insight, but rather by customer segments, markets, brands, products or delivery channels.

Segmentation is often a hot topic in marketing circles, both within businesses where competing factions may have their own preferences for how segmentation should be done, and in academia where experts like Byron Sharp have questioned the way that segmentation is deployed. The IMA is critical of quite a lot of segmentation, but a really key benefit of good segmentation is to provide a framework into which you can then add new knowledge.

If you have identified an important group of consumers who purchase a disproportionate amount of one product, then adding new insight about this segment to your existing knowledge base becomes a key part of your Insight agenda. If, by contrast, you have no organising framework to codify your insights, then you are likely to end up with a mush of apparently contradictory findings and a very poor crop to harvest.

A critical aspect of knowledge cultivation is conversation between Insight professionals. If you have team meetings where all you ever do is report on project progress, you are wasting a wonderful opportunity to develop knowledge and collective understanding. Encourage your colleagues to talk about their findings on a regular basis; not only will this help the projects themselves – because many heads are better than one – but it also helps to re-inforce the fundamental truths that provide context for everything else. Or to challenge them: misconceptions, out of date assumptions, partial truths... their weaknesses often come to light when Insight professionals start talking to each other.

By constantly reviewing what we know, prioritising it by relative importance, codifying it by customer segment, market, brand, product and channel, and then discussing the emerging knowledge base and adding fresh perspectives, Insight teams begin to create an asset of real value. They can also start to develop an Insight farming mindset. When you adopt this, you stop thinking about new requests and new projects in isolation; instead you see them as the next opportunity to grow your big picture understanding of how and why consumers in your market become customers of your organisation and create or destroy value for it.

....

The 9th secret of successful Insight teams is that they actively cultivate structured customer knowledge

If you would like to explore this topic further, you might like to read the IMA's Insight leader guide *IMP203: How to cultivate customer knowledge*

....

Key points to consider:

1. The first stages of Insight farming may be as simple as gathering together the best pieces of work you have done
2. But knowledge cultivation really takes off when you codify your learning by customer segment, market, brand, product and channel
3. Customer segmentation plays a vital role in knowledge cultivation, providing the hooks on which you can hang new learning
4. Insight leaders should always encourage their teams to talk about what they know and the new things they observe
5. With a farming mindset you see every project as an opportunity to grow your knowledge base and improve the Insight ecosystem

The best Insight projects start with an appreciation of what is known so far and what new pieces of the jigsaw now need to be added; they end with another valuable contribution to the Insight team's ever-expanding knowledge base. But where do we file new insights and build this asset? That's the topic we'll look at in the next chapter, the final one in this section.

Chapter 10
Developing systems

In the last three chapters I've been exploring the importance of accumulating insights and developing a customer and market knowledge base. But we've barely mentioned one aspect that many researchers and analysts would probably suggest first when talking about knowledge: systems.

Knowledge systems are an integral part of many Insight teams' evolution, and some of the systems available today are extremely sophisticated. They offer a wide range of functionality, from logging Insight requests, project management, recording findings, and smart search and retrieval capabilities; the most sophisticated now use artificial intelligence to bring back relevant material. Some can be very expensive (at least in terms of Insight capability) and many are beautifully packaged and a delight to work with.

So why wait until this, the tenth chapter of a book called *Transforming Insight*, to talk about them?

Over that last fifteen years the IMA has talked to hundreds of Insight leaders, visited its members' offices, and discussed the systems they wish they had, would love to afford, were developing, embedding, or replacing. And the aspect of these conversation that always stands out is that it's not really about the systems themselves, brilliant though some of them are; it's about identifying what role you need systems to play if you are going to make

Insight make a difference in your organisation. The smartest systems are no replacement for developing an acute understanding of Insight's purpose and role in your company; acting as consultants to nail and map the key business issues; approaching Insight investigations like forensic detectives; and farming insight to cultivate knowledge. Systems are a means to an end. So that's why I've talked about some of those ends first.

What support do Insight teams need from systems?

There are many aspects to identify, so here's a starter for ten focusing on the non-technical aspects of Insight systems:

Insight knowledge systems do not have to be very sophisticated. If you were tempted to skip this chapter because your company isn't going to give you $100k to build or buy the system you saw demonstrated at a research conference last week, don't worry. Some really good Insight teams have managed for years with well-organised shared drives, lists of projects in Excel spreadsheets, and hyperlinks to project reports. The important thing is to think through processes that will support the aims we've discussed in the chapters so far, and then use the budget you have available to develop systems that will support them.

Work with your organisation, not against it. Many companies have restrictions in place that prohibit the adoption of commercially available third-party systems, so use what you can. For some that means standard Microsoft products, or piggy-backing on the company intranet. Several IMA members have developed extremely good knowledge management systems using Microsoft SharePoint because that was their company's chosen platform for intranet sites. Another tip is to align your Insight portals with Internal Communications teams and other 'official' sources of corporate knowledge.

Insight systems often serve more than one purpose, and they often have more than one user group. Classically there are:

- **Internal users** – in other words the Insight team themselves who want to record requests, file their project findings, and have a quick way to retrieve accumulated insight when beginning new research or analysis.

- **External users** – your colleagues in other departments who want to log requests for the Insight team's support, check on project progress, and self-serve by finding the results of previous projects. It can also include third party agencies if you give them access.

Start with the Insight team's own needs first. That might sound odd, but it's because no matter how many brand managers and marketing executives sign up for email alerts when you post new documents on your portal, or browse the latest reports looking for inspiration, it is nearly always the Insight team itself that will be the most frequent user of any knowledge system you develop.

Think hard about the level of insights that you want to record, and make sure that this is consistent with the purpose and culture of your Insight team. If it's your team mission to democratise data, then by all means focus on ways to give your colleagues in other departments access to customer and market data itself, with maybe the capability to build their own dashboards, or have a sandbox in which they can carry out safe analysis. But if you've decided that your Insight team's focus is to provide evidence-based opinions about customers and markets, then think carefully before providing unfettered access to raw data.

Many knowledge management systems work at a project level; they are effectively systems for recording and retrieving lists of projects that have been carried out. That's OK in itself, but if you want to provide opinions based on accumulated insight rather than individual insights, you're going to need documents that provide a summary of that accumulated knowledge and signpost users to that first. You will need a system that allows the recording and retrieval of *insight*, not just *insights*.

Time spent tagging is never wasted. The latest knowledge systems have far better search functionality than ever before, but anything that you can do to categorise and summarise the learning using the frameworks we discussed in the last chapter (customer segment, market, brand, product, channel) will help the Insight team and other colleagues to find what they really need.

It's all about usability, and at this stage in our book we're going to focus on usability for the Insight team itself. If you don't get buy-in from your Insight colleagues to use systems in a consistent way, you're wasting all the time and money you put into those systems. Sometimes it's enough for an Insight leader to issue a command... but in most companies it's going to take persuasion and consideration of the behavioural biases that will drive or thwart adoption. If nothing else, make your systems easy to use, attractive to use, socially acceptable, and available to use quickly at the right time.

....

The 10th secret of successful Insight teams is that they adopt systems to support knowledge management and development

If you would like to explore this topic further, you might like to read the IMA's Insight leader guide *IMP204: How to adopt knowledge systems*

....

Key points to consider:

1. Insight team purpose, role and ways of working should drive the adoption of knowledge systems, not vice versa

2. If your budget doesn't stretch to a sophisticated system you can often achieve similar aims with far less spend

3. Make use of the platforms favoured by the rest of your company; piggy-back on group intranet sites or Internal Communication sites

4. Focus on recording insights and insight at a level that is consistent with your team purpose and way of working

5. It's all about the people: systems will be as useful or useless as the level of engagement you get from your Insight colleagues

In this first section, *Identifying Value*, I have concentrated on the Insight team itself: its purpose, ways of working, and culture. But there is no point identifying how your company could create more value if nobody then does anything about it. So the ten chapters of the next section of this book are going to focus on the audience for your insight, and the ways in which you can engage them to drive change.

Section 2

Driving change within our organisations

Driving change within our organisations

In the second section of *Transforming Insight*, we will focus on the second ten secrets of successful corporate Insight teams:

Chapter 11
Driving change through influence

The first section of this book explored the twin requirements for corporate Insight teams to generate new insights and develop accumulated knowledge about their customers, their markets and their own business. I suggested that if we want to transform our Insight teams, then not only do we have to change our mindset about research and analysis projects, but we have to re-balance our focus from Insight generation to Insight farming.

However, there is no point in either generating new insights nor farming customer knowledge if our organisations continue to behave in the same way as they would have done without us doing our work. An Insight team needs to identify valuable opportunities for its company, but then also drive the corporate changes necessary to profit from those opportunities.

At this point you may be asking, 'isn't it enough just to produce great insights?' Unfortunately, it isn't. A great insight poorly communicated will sink without trace, whilst a reasonable insight brilliantly communicated can spread like wildfire. How we disseminate our knowledge and ideas is at least as important as how we generate them, so in the second section of this book I'm going to make the case for an even bigger re-balancing of our time and resources.

Two ways to drive change

Over the last 15 years, the IMA has formed the view that there are two very different ways in which Insight teams can drive change:

First, let's think about supply and demand. On the supply side, we are trying to build Insight teams that have both lots of new insights to share, but also an abundance of big picture knowledge and opinions. On the demand side, many of us work for large, complex organisations that will take lots of decisions every day that affect customers and the propositions we offer them. If our Insight teams are going to meet this complex organisational demand with the rich understanding we can supply, then we need to consider a wide-scale knowledge dissemination programme, and a complimentary focus on key communication skills.

But before we look at the broad topic of Insight communication in more detail, we need to recognise that Pareto's law applies to corporate decision-making just like it applies to many aspects of business life. 80% of big decisions will be taken by 20% of senior executives (at most!) so we all need to give a disproportionate amount of our attention to influencing that senior group of managers.

How can we influence senior decision-makers?

I suspect a lot of Insight professionals would be tempted to say, 'with difficulty!' and I've got a lot of sympathy with that. On the one hand, many large organisations in the commercial and public sector do not take decisions very well and their default position is to accommodate only a fragmented view of their customers and markets. But the blame also lies with us: market researchers and customer analysts tend to be recruited, developed and promoted for their technical skills, and too little focus is placed on our colleagues' ability to drive change.

This is particularly true when it comes to influencing senior people. I said in the last section that some Insight specialists are reluctant to interpret data, and many hesitate to form an opinion based on their interpretation. Therefore, it's not surprising if a significant proportion of our people will instinctively hide under their desks when we ask them to knock on senior executives' doors and sell their ideas.

The answer is not to beat people up or force them out of their comfort zones. Over a period of time I think we need to reconsider what skills and attributes we recruit for in the first place, and we'll look at this aspect later in the book. But here and now the IMA believes there's a series of things that all Insight leaders can consider, things that have been seen to make a difference in organisations in the UK, North America and Europe where Insight teams are most effective.

Top tips for Insight leaders

The first aspect to consider is the needs of those we are trying to influence. As Insight teams we spend a lot of our time reminding our organisations that we all need to understand consumers better before we can persuade them to do more business with us. But the same is true within a company as well: we cannot improve our influencing unless we first improve our understanding. So, ironically, Insight teams need to develop better insights about our key stakeholders. We will explore this in chapter 12.

Second, we all know that personally we are most likely to be influenced by those we like, know well, and trust. We may have observed that senior people at work frequently seem to be surrounded by a small group of trusted advisers, often those who report directly to them, but maybe supplemented by consultants, strategists, finance people and HR managers. They develop their own inner circle. Ultimately Insight leaders and their teams would be far more influential if we were invited to join that inner circle, so we'll look at this in chapter 13.

Third, whilst many members of our teams will have specific development needs when it comes to influencing, there are some common needs often found amongst the introverts who tend to form a larger part of analysis and research teams than they do of other departments. We'll explore influencing skills for introverts in chapter 14.

Finally, we need to be pragmatic and recognise that we can't know everything about our stakeholders that we'd like to; nor instantly form close relationships with them; nor immediately transform our introverts' comfort with influencing. But we can quickly learn how to be canny by looking at the behavioural biases shown by decision-makers and coming up with ideas for how we might 'nudge' them. Many Insight teams are becoming behavioural economics evangelists because of the paramount importance of understanding why consumers really make the purchase decisions they do. Now it's time we developed a behavioural economics playbook for influencing within our own companies, so we'll explore this in chapter 15.

....

The 11th secret of successful Insight teams is that they drive change through influencing senior decision-makers

If you would like to explore this topic further, you might like to read the IMA's Insight leader guide *IMP301: An introduction to Insight influence*

....

Key points to consider:

1. There is no point generating new insights unless something changes in your organisation as a result
2. If an organisation aspires to be customer-centric then everyone in an organisation ought to know about customers and markets
3. However, the Insight team should focus first on influencing the small number of senior executives who make the biggest decisions
4. Insight professionals tend to be recruited and promoted due to their technical skills and may be uncomfortable with influencing
5. Insight leaders should seek to improve both their team's strategic influencing skills and their tactical ability to nudge stakeholders

We cannot influence unless we first understand, so before you read further, stop and think about how well your Insight team really understands its decision-makers. That's the topic we'll look at in the next chapter.

Chapter 12
Seek first to understand

What question do you get asked most often at work? Is it about what insights we have on our customers? Or about the latest insights on our brand? Or perhaps it's about insight on the latest consumer trend?

Every organisation has its own hot topics, and every Insight team could compile a list of their most frequently asked questions. But how often do we ask ourselves about the insight which we have on the audience for our own work – the senior decision-makers in our organisation?

Just like a company needs to understand its external customers if it's going to influence their behaviour, so our Insight teams need to understand our internal customers if we're going to influence their decisions. We all tell our organisations to spend more time really understanding customers. How well do we practice what we preach?

Do we really understand decision-makers?

One of the benefits of working in Customer Insight roles is that we often get the chance to develop years of expertise in the tools of our trade. Some of us become expert market researchers, others focus on analysis, others on desk research, competitors, or broader trend monitoring.

But a disadvantage of these years of Insight experience is that there's a good chance that we won't have spent much time in decision-making roles ourselves. Furthermore, in larger companies we will often be surrounded by other Insight specialists, which is great for sharing technical knowledge and market understanding, but unfortunately it can isolate us from the world of our senior decision-makers.

So let's take some time out to think about our internal audience, about the world in which they live, about the way they make their decisions, and what it feels like to make those decisions.

Do we really understand decision-makers?

Senior directors are working ever longer hours, they are having to sift through unbelievable amounts of information, and they are changing roles more frequently. Every time they make a decision they are not only taking a business risk that may result in lost sales, revenue or reputation; they are also taking a personal risk with their careers, with the reputation they have built amongst colleagues, and of course with their own sense of success or failure.

In this environment many executives default to consulting trusted advisers from their own departments, or making decisions unduly influenced by their personal, and often narrow, experience. That's not surprising: we'd do the same thing ourselves. But if we would like to see ourselves as internal consultants to senior stakeholders, I think we need to demonstrate a lot more empathy with them.

In his famous book, *The 7 Habits of Highly Effective People*, Stephen Covey advises us all to 'seek first to understand, then to be understood'. This doesn't mean abandoning our Insight perspective or putting aside the passionate opinions we've developed based on our customer knowledge. But it does mean demonstrating a lot more empathy with our senior colleagues and getting a far better feel for both their rational and emotional needs.

The IMA believes that all progressive Insight teams should develop:

- Understanding about what it's like to make big decisions in today's environment, complete with its stresses and time pressures

- Knowledge of the individual decision-makers we seek to influence: their priorities, personality types, communication preferences

The better we understand the world of senior decision-makers in general, the more likely we are to appreciate what they need from us. This understanding provides a good foundation for building relationships, but then of course we have to overlay more specific knowledge of what makes individual stakeholders tick and reflect on whether there are things about our personality styles and communication preferences which are at odds with theirs.

Over the last 15 years the IMA's consultants have visited many Insight teams and talked to them about personal styles and communication preferences. A common finding is that there are often pronounced differences between analysts and researchers within teams, and between both these groups and the marketing teams and wider organisations in which they work. As with all work on personality types, it's not that one type is right and another wrong, rather that all our types have strengths and weaknesses, and these tend to be compounded when the departments in which we work have a structural bias towards people who are quite like us.

The key learnings are to become more aware of your own style and other people's, and to reflect on the ways in which differences in style have an impact on communication. We should also consider the issue of translation: Insight teams have a tendency to speak their own language with technical terms about research or analysis, customer and market metrics. These all have their place, but we need to translate them into the language understood by our audience: the language of sales, operations, revenue and costs.

....

The 12th secret of successful Insight teams is that they develop insights about their organisation's decision-makers

If you would like to explore this topic further, you might like to read the IMA's Insight leader guide *IMP302: How to understand decision-makers*

....

Key points to consider:

1. Insight teams often have relatively little insight about the internal consumers of our own Insight work
2. As Stephen Covey observed, before we can hope to be understood ourselves, we should seek first to understand others
3. Insight teams would benefit from a better appreciation of the business and personal risks involved in taking big decisions
4. We should also develop better understanding about specific decision-makers, their personalities and communication preferences
5. Insight teams need to translate their customer and market knowledge into the language used by the rest of the business

I hope that Insight managers, corporate researchers and analysts reading this will feel some reassurance: the influencing journey starts with some new pieces of insight! But based on insights we have to drive change, and this time the change is going to be in ourselves, as we'll see in the next chapter.

Chapter 14
Improving stakeholder relationships

The most progressive Insight teams would all recognise that they are on a journey from being reactive service providers to key business partners. They want to influence decision-makers and their decisions. They want to be included early in discussions about business challenges and to be valued for their opinions, experience and input. They don't want to be called in late in the day, with insights merely being used to rubber-stamp decisions that have already been taken.

In the last chapter I suggested that we would never influence any group of people before we had taken steps to better understand them, and that most Insight teams could improve the insight they had regarding the internal audience for their work. But having taken steps to better understand decision-makers in general, and our key stakeholders in particular, we then need to put those insights into action and drive change within our Insight teams.

So far the steps we have explored to transform Insight have focused mainly on whole-team mindset and whole-team behaviours. This next step is also one for the whole team to embrace, but the nature of the challenge itself is probably more personal than most of the ones we've looked at so far. It could well be the biggest challenge yet for some of your colleagues.

We all know people who are natural relationship-builders, people who find their own way to win friends and influence people. We may have observed particular things that they have done and tried to learn from the tips they have given us. One example that sticks in my mind was a colleague who many years ago realised that senior management had a perception that his team were always inclined to say 'no' and were seen as natural blockers to things that others wanted to change. So he decided that from then on he was going to say 'yes' to everything. Now that wasn't as reckless as it sounds, because he made sure that he made people aware of the implications if he did exactly as they asked him to, but every time he explained the negative consequences of a course of action, he made a positive suggestion for how the business could take a slightly different decision and avoid the potential problems. By changing his default response to 'yes, we could do that for you' he framed the subsequent interaction in a far more positive way and it quickly shaped the stakeholders' perception of him and his team as problem-solvers not business blockers.

But not everyone can find their own way to behaviour change like this, and some of us will just find it difficult to be influencers at work. So let's think about who influences us in our own personal lives and why we find those people so persuasive.

Whose advice are we most likely to take?

If I asked you whose advice you are most likely to accept, you'll probably think about two groups of people. On the one hand there are the family and friends who are obviously on our side and who would always consider our best interests. Then there are people whose authority you accept on a particular subject, especially those who are adept at sharing their knowledge in a way that makes sense to us. The perfect combination are people we like and who we also think are more knowledgeable than us on the subject in question. Our opinions are often shaped by theirs without us even realising it. We all constantly buy the messenger not the message.

Conversely, we are far less likely to be influenced by those we instinctively distrust, or people we don't know well enough to judge whether we can trust them or not. We are far more likely to question the advice itself if it comes from a source whose wisdom we question, or whom we suspect may have a motive other than helping us to solve our problem. Once we have doubts about the advice-giver it can be very difficult for us to listen to the advice even if sometimes it is objectively right. This applies at both an individual and category level: how do you pick out the genuine bargain when a used-car salesman is in full flow, or make an objective decision about pension provision if you distrust the financial adviser sitting in front of you?

The way that influence works in the workplace has far more in common with the way it works in our personal lives than we often assume. People buy from people just as much between 9am and 5pm Monday to Friday as they do in their home life at the weekends. Therefore, if we want to influence senior people and drive change with our insights, we need to appreciate that it's no good just working on making our insights better, we also need to work on other people's perceptions of us both as individuals and as a department.

How can Insight professionals become trusted advisers?

The IMA's best practice work suggests Insight teams should aspire to be trusted advisers to the senior decision-makers in our organisations. The phrase 'trusted adviser' is used quite commonly by those seeking to influence others, but it was also given a more specific definition by Maister, Green and Galford in their book, *The Trusted Advisor*, in 2000. This was initially written to guide professional advisers in the USA, but we believe that it's highly relevant for aspiring Insight teams worldwide.

Maister, Green and Galford say that to become trusted advisers we should first work on our *trustworthiness* which they say is built by conveying credibility and reliability, and an appropriate degree of intimacy. However, all this can be undermined if we are seen to be self-orientated, in other words driven by what's best for us not the person we advise. You can't make someone trust you at work any more than you can make someone love you at home. But you can take a disciplined approach to making yourself *trustworthy*. So what practical steps can we take? Taking our cue from Maister, Green and Galford, we should work on our:

Credibility: Many analysts and researchers already have credibility in the eyes of senior managers, but if this credibility largely rests on their technical expertise in 'doing analysis' or 'doing research' then it's time for us to figure out how to build our credibility as people who can apply customer knowledge to solve business problems.

Reliability: All Insight specialists want to be seen as reliable, but there is always scope for improving the way we manage expectations and build a track record for delivering what has been promised, on time, every time.

Intimacy: The concept of intimacy in a professional workplace is more of a challenge for some, but there are steps we can all take to consider other people's feelings and to be more open about our own.

Self-orientation: This takes conscious effort: it can be difficult to recognise self-orientation unless we consciously reflect on our own behaviour and the way we approach conversations with stakeholders.

....

The 13th secret of successful Insight teams is that they seek to become trusted advisers to senior decision-makers

If you would like to explore this topic further, you might like to read the IMA's Insight leader guide *IMP303: How to improve stakeholder relationships*

....

Key points to consider:

1. Corporate Insight professionals should work on their reputation as messengers as well as on the messages they convey

2. We should seek ways to build our credibility as business advisers

3. We should actively develop our reputation for reliability

4. We should be more open to sharing our feelings and personalities and recognise the importance of knowing colleagues on a personal level

5. We should reflect on the things that we do subconsciously that make us appear self-orientated, either as individuals or as a department

Several times in this book I've drawn attention to the distinction between extroverts and introverts, and the particular issues that this can raise for Insight teams. I think this is especially an issue with influencing, so in the next chapter we're going to explore that topic in more detail.

Chapter 14
Influence skills for introverts

It's 11am on Friday morning, three hours before my weekly 121 with my line manager. I've got a whole pile of work to finish before the weekend, and now I've got that to look forward to! Great...

What will she ask me to do today? There'll be a discussion about the market share analysis I've been working on, of course. Just remembered that she's away on holiday next week... hope she doesn't ask me to deputise for her and present it to the board! Then there's the analysis I've just done on product sales by segment. Really enjoyed working on that one, but now she'll have another go at me for not having arranged a face-to-face meeting with the product director to discuss it.

And then there's that market research conference she was talking about at the team meeting yesterday. She was asking for volunteers, and when she looked around the table and said that some of us really must improve our networking skills, I had a horrible feeling she might be thinking about volunteering me for it. Great! Can't wait...

Working in a world shaped by extroverts

It's confession time: I'm an introvert. Nothing unusual in that, of course. Psychologists think that about one in three of the population are more introvert than extrovert, and informal surveys and discussions at the

Insight forum in London suggest that it's a far higher proportion of Insight specialists.

The technical distinction between extroverts and introverts isn't about how loud someone likes to be. It's more to do with the source of our energy and inspiration. Is our natural tendency to talk to the person next to us if we are stuck? Or to go for a walk on our own and reflect in silence?

There's a continuum here of course, but analysis at Barclays some years ago showed that there were far more natural introverts in the Insight team than there were in the marketing department or in the C-suite. The skew was most pronounced in the customer analysis division, where there was a far higher degree of introversion than in the market research division.

The exact mix of introverts and extroverts in your team might well be affected by your ratio of analysts to market researchers. Analysts and quantitative researchers are the most likely to be introverts, our personality type often well suited to reflection and critical thinking. But all types of Insight expert are more likely to be introverts than our marketing neighbours – and of course the leadership group that we report to and seek to influence.

Corporate life isn't always very comfortable for introverts. The problem is not us; the problem is that many of the working practices that have developed in our offices over the last few decades implicitly favour extroverts over introverts. Let's think about the things we take for granted: Designing a new office? Let's make it open plan. Need new ideas for a project? Let's have a team brainstorm. Want to increase your chances of promotion? Volunteer to deliver a high-profile presentation. Attending a conference to learn about market research? Let's build in plenty of time for participants to network with their peers.

Writers such as Susan Cain have highlighted the extent to which our standard approaches to many of these issues sometimes feel like they have been invented by extroverts for other extroverts. They can leave introverts – or anyone who is just naturally shy or lacking in social confidence – feeling very uncomfortable.

How can introverts thrive in an extrovert world?

The IMA's Julia Joskey has been examining this topic, and in particular the issue of how we Insight leaders can get the most from the introverts in our teams. The first thing to recognise is that there are plenty of situations where introverts tend to have a natural advantage. Examples might be really listening to customers and reflecting on their needs; or critically examining the options when we're facing a thorny business problem.

But in order to get the most out of all our team members and make sure that we are not subconsciously discriminating against introverts, Insight leaders should reflect on the social aspect of the tasks we expect our analysts and researchers to perform. This relates in particular to influencing skills: how do we square the introvert / extrovert mix in our team with the demands that we have just said in previous chapters we want to place on our teams to become better business influencers?

Top tips for Insight leaders:

- Start by simply recognising that a significant number of your Insight colleagues will instinctively feel uncomfortable at the idea of influencing senior managers

- Take care not to subconsciously discriminate by assuming that everyone wants to spend time networking with other departments

- Consider the social demands of making presentations, arranging meetings and picking up the phone; is there anything that the extroverts can do to help the introverts?

- Try to find ways of playing to your colleagues' strengths and give introverts responsibility for listening to stakeholders, reflecting on their needs, and drawing up plans for how the overall department can become more persuasive

- Over a period of time, there may be things that you can do to help all your colleagues to grow in social confidence in the workplace. But we may also have to recognise that to drive change you need to alter the mix of introverts and extroverts in your Insight team

Above all, let's be more considerate. Next time we find ourselves complaining about some of our colleagues' inability to communicate as well as we would like them to – 'my biggest problem is just getting my analysts to talk to the rest of the business' – we should reflect on what might be driving that behaviour, and then think about how we could help the situation by changing our own behaviour.

....

The 14th secret of successful Insight teams is that they learn how to harness the power of their introverts

If you would like to explore this topic further, you might like to read the IMA's Insight leader guide IMP304: Influencing skills for introverts

....

Key points to consider:

1. Insight teams tend to contain more introverts than most other corporate departments, especially those with lots of analysts
2. Marketing departments and the senior leadership group we seek to influence will probably contain a higher proportion of extroverts
3. Many of the working practices that have developed in our offices over the last few decades implicitly favour extroverts over introverts
4. Many introverts feel uncomfortable when faced with the challenge of influencing others
5. However, there are aspects to influencing that introverts are naturally very good at so let's make sure we get the best out of everyone

The last three chapters have looked at strategic ways of making our Insight teams drive change by becoming better business influencers. But sometimes we just need to be canny with our tactics, so that's what we'll look at in the next chapter.

Chapter 15
Nudging decision-makers

The last 20 years have seen an enormous advance in humans' understanding of our own psychology. Some of the most notable progress has involved deep analysis of the way we make decisions, and an entire field of study – and a whole library of popular books – now focuses on the topic of behavioural economics (BE).

Classical economic theory assumes that humans always make rational decisions, especially when we spend money. Economic models and textbooks have usually assumed that we always make decisions which are:

- Rational - we consider all options regardless of how they are presented, so context doesn't matter
- Self-interested - we consider only what is right for us, so we have no feelings of obligation to others or the person presenting the options to us
- Maximise utility - what we physically end up with is what matters to us, not how that choice makes us feel

As an example, classical economic theory would predict that after a meal in a restaurant, we would act in our own economic self-interest by accepting the free mints on offer with the bill, without that having any impact on our decision about whether to leave a tip.

However, behavioural economists have shown how in practice this and many, many other textbook assumptions are simply not true. During the course of every day we repeatedly do things that are not perfectly rational, nor necessarily in our own interest. But just because our behaviour is not rational, that does not make it random. In fact, experiments have shown that our choices are guided by a long list of behavioural biases, and a good knowledge of these can have the effect of making us 'predictably irrational'.

So what has all this got to do with the world of corporate Insight? Well, for starters, anyone who has ever been involved with market research will know that there has always been a gap between what consumers claim is important, and what they actually do when you can observe their behaviour. As David Ogilvy is reported to have said, 'The trouble with market research is that people don't think what they feel, they don't say what they think, and they don't do what they say'. We are not good at analysing ourselves, we post-rationalise or provide what we feel are socially acceptable answers. To get round these issues many Insight teams and research agencies have adopted key learning from behavioural economics and applied it to their own work with consumers.

However, the IMA believes that our corporate Insight teams need to pay just as much attention to understanding senior stakeholders as they do to understanding the company's end customers. If we don't know how corporate decisions are taken in our own head office, we stand little chance of influencing those decisions. And if we don't influence those decisions, there was no point in doing any analysis or research on consumers in the first place.

Therefore we feel that the advent of behavioural economics could be the biggest thing to happen to the fields of analysis, research and Insight in forty years, potentially even more significant than the arrival of big data.

How can Insight teams nudge decision-makers?

A knowledge of behavioural biases can be just as useful to Insight teams who want to influence their stakeholders as to those who want to learn more about the drivers of consumer choice. It can help us to develop a list of handy tactics which we can use, almost irrespective of how well we know the decision-makers concerned.

The IMA see this as a parallel and complimentary approach to understanding decision-makers and building better relationships with them. We all know that we are likely to have more influence with those who see us as trusted advisers, so earning senior executives' trust should be a strategic aim for all those in corporate Insight departments. But this does not mean that it doesn't also pay to be canny on occasion; we can't suddenly become trusted advisers overnight to everyone who has asked for Insight's support.

And the two approaches can work well in combination with each other. Every parent knows that there are times when they may have to deploy clever tactics to influence their children to eat properly, tidy their rooms or do their homework. Merely having a great relationship with someone is sometimes not enough!

But it is not necessary for everyone to suddenly acquaint themselves with all 170 behavioural biases (or however many you can now find on Google). Instead, consider using the EAST framework developed by the UK Government's Behavioural Insights Team (popularly known as the Nudge Unit) and consider how you could present findings and options to decision-makers such that they were:

Easy: if you want to encourage people to do something, make it as easy for them as possible to take that decision

Attractive: if you want to encourage people to do something, make the process by which the decision is made attractive or rewarding

Social: if you want to encourage people to do something, tap into how people are influenced by other people and their reactions to our choices

Timely: if you want to encourage people to do something, target them at the right moment and use time-related motivators

The UK Nudge Unit have used this framework to categorise the specific behavioural biases, but there is a lot of merit in keeping things simple to start with and just using the four EAST factors themselves. But using a simple framework does not remove the need to analyse how decisions are taken; we have to map the process involved from when information is presented to when choices are made, then figure out how we can make the communication of our findings more appealing and the acceptance of our recommendations more likely.

....

The 15th secret of successful Insight teams is that they use learning from behavioural economics to nudge decision-makers

If you would like to explore this topic further, you might like to read the IMA's Insight leader guide *IMP305: Behavioural economics for Insight teams* and *IMP306: How to nudge decision-makers*

....

Key points to consider:

1. In both our personal lives and our corporate decisions human beings are not rational, but predictably irrational
2. Many Insight teams are embracing behavioural economics to learn more about consumer choices and ways to nudge them
3. But BE also presents us with a great opportunity to nudge our senior decision-makers, regardless of how well we know them
4. There are many relevant biases, and all Insight professionals should seek a basic understanding of some of the most important
5. A quick win is to focus on making it easier, more attractive, socially acceptable, and timely for senior people to accept the advice we give

If we are going to drive change we need to influence the people at the top of our organisation, but there are so many other colleagues whose performance could be improved if they understood more about our customers. How can we better share our knowledge with them? That's the topic we'll look at in the next chapter.

Chapter 16
Driving change through communication

Organisations invest money in Insight functions in order to improve their performance. In a commercial organisation, that means adding sustainable profits to the bottom line; in a public sector organisation, that might mean delivering better value for money; and in a charity, raising income and improving the outcomes achieved.

The day-to-day activity of Insight teams can sometimes seem far removed from this. We spend much of our time doing pieces of analysis, investigating changes in customer behaviour, or managing market research projects. These things are fascinating and many of us were drawn to Insight in the first place because we get a lot of intellectual satisfaction from them. They all have their role to play as key inputs to the Insight generation process.

As Insight professionals, we would often like to think that the sheer beauty of our insights will be enough to convince senior executives to do something differently. But the reality is that the way we share our knowledge is at least as important as the insights themselves. As one member of the IMA's Insight forum put it many years ago, a great insight badly communicated will sink without trace, but a reasonable insight, brilliantly communicated, will spread like wildfire throughout your organisation.

In the last five chapters we've focused on how to influence the very senior people in each company who make many of the key decisions because that's usually the best way to achieve the most impact.

But if your company aspires to be truly customer-centric, then it follows that there will be far more employees who need to understand key aspects of customer relationships, behaviour, and its drivers than you could possibly talk to. Insight teams cannot be present in every discussion that affects corporate decisions. But insights and insight – the results of our work – can be present if an Insight team has a proper communication programme, a clear focus on disseminating knowledge, on structuring messages, storytelling and visualisation.

Some Insight professionals really enjoy communication. There are market researchers who love telling stories, and analysts who enjoy creating infographics almost as much as doing the customer and market analysis itself. But in most Insight teams in the UK, Europe and North America, the communication of insight tends to be bolted onto projects as an after-thought, and little or no attention is given to developing a comprehensive communication programme. In this chapter and the next four I hope to inspire Insight leaders to take communication far more seriously, and introduce frameworks that can help our team members to develop key skills.

Top tips for Insight leaders

If we are to share our knowledge and ideas more effectively, perhaps we need to forget that it's usually our day job to run research projects and manage teams of analysts. We should stop thinking like Insight leaders altogether and think like the IMA's six characters of Insight communication:

Think like a chief marketing officer... to plan your Insight team's programme of communication. Consider the audiences, the content, and the channels through which you can share your knowledge. Do you show videos of customer interviews in your elevators? In your staff restaurants? At offsite meetings and in senior leaders' presentations? Do you use gamification, postcards, posters, life-sized images of customer personas? How professional is your Insight intranet site? Does it make people want to click on it every week and read more? Do you have a multi-channel communication strategy, or do you just stick it in PowerPoint and hope someone is listening?

Think like a consultant... in Chapter 5 we looked at the SCQAB way of structuring Insight projects. The good news is that this also works brilliantly for pieces of Insight communication. Start each presentation with a clear statement of the Situation, the Complications which have led to the research, and the key business Questions which this raises. Make sure you can provide joined-up Answers to those questions, and don't forget to spell out the Benefits to the business if they adopt your ideas.

Think like an author... storytelling is all the rage in big business today, but unfortunately many storytelling workshops leave us feeling unsure how to apply the key principles back to our day jobs. But that doesn't mean that it's not relevant to us. We all need to focus on a key message and work out the most engaging way to communicate it.

Think like a journalist... spend time crafting headlines to hook your audience, use emotion and real life situations to create interest and curiosity. Does your work make an impact? Does it leave an impression?

Think like an editor... because most of what you put in your first draft deserves to be discarded. Keep it simple, use signposts and key facts, ask others to go through your work before publishing it, because we are all poor editors of our own writing.

Think like a designer... because a picture can tell a thousand words, but only if your imagery is as simple, clear and focused as your narrative.

....

The 16th secret of successful Insight teams is that they recognise that communicating insights is as important as generating them.

If you would like to explore this topic further, you might like to read the IMA's Insight leader guide *IMP401: An introduction to Insight communication*

....

Key points to consider:

1. A great insight badly communicated will sink without trace, but a reasonable insight, well communicated, will spread like wildfire
2. Insight teams tend to give too little attention to developing a comprehensive communication programme
3. All pieces of communication need to have a clear structure to make it easy to navigate the messages and follow the narrative
4. Storytelling is a key skill for Insight professionals but will only improve if we find better ways to make it relevant to our roles
5. A picture can tell a thousand words, but only if your imagery is as simple, clear and focused as your narrative

This chapter has introduced the six characters of Insight communication. In the next four chapters we will spend some time with them all, starting with the CMO. Many of the principles they use for marketing communication apply equally to internal communication, so we'll look at some of these in the next chapter.

Chapter 17
The Insight communication programme

Many corporate Insight teams work very closely with marketing departments, but how good are we at marketing our own insights? Or even recognising the need to market them?

When Insight leaders think about improving the communication of their knowledge and ideas, they normally focus on team skills and behaviour. These are really important of course, but a focus only on skills can lead to piecemeal improvement in how some topics are communicated without a top down plan for what is to be communicated, when and to whom.

This is a really big issue for Insight teams because, as we saw in chapter 7, most of our teams' time and money tends to be spent on individual projects. Very few Insight teams around the world yet have enough focus on joining the dots between projects and developing an accumulated body of knowledge about key markets, segments, products, brands and channels.

If our Insight communication is also piecemeal, it reinforces the tendency to provide our company with fragmented insights.

Stepping away from our normal way of doing things, let's consider how a chief marketing officer (CMO) might approach this challenge. They would put a lot of effort into individual TV adverts, social media or email campaigns. But they would also recognise the need for a company to plan a communication programme for its customers and prospects to make sure that the marketing department is prioritising the right messages, to the right audiences, at the right time, and in a way most likely to change behaviour.

How might our Insight teams benefit from this approach? I think it would start with a focus on three key elements of communication planning: audiences, content and channels.

Audiences: any piece of communication should start by considering the audience, and so should a communication plan. Who are the audiences that would benefit from seeing more customer and market insight within the organisation? There are probably many, ranging from the boardroom to operations and customer-facing roles. We're really interested in anyone who is in position to make decisions that affect how our company's products and services are designed, promoted and delivered to customers.

Content: which individual insights and pieces of accumulated understanding would these very different audiences find most useful? This might vary by product or brand, or by the level of detail which it was appropriate to communicate. Generally speaking, the more senior the audience, the shorter the attention span, so the greater the focus on synthesising complex topics. Rather than push the same content to everyone, can we research the needs of different groups of colleagues – a radical idea for an Insight team! – and maybe define a 'target knowledge state'; who ought to know what?

Channels: how can we deliver different types of message to different audiences? Can we move away from PowerPoint, Excel and Word, and think about video, animation, intranet portals, competitions, postcards, posters, physical objects, town hall meetings or brown bag lunches?

Intranet portals are a particularly hot topic for many Insight teams. As we discussed in chapter 10, it is the Insight team itself who will always be the biggest user of knowledge portals, but many of the same systems that we can use to store, structure and share work amongst ourselves also present fantastic opportunities for allowing some of our audiences to self-serve and explore content for themselves. It goes without saying, however, that the more we want our audiences to be self-sufficient, the more thought we have to give to synthesising, curating, tagging and editing the material that we make available online.

Although most communication plans quite rightly start with the audience, there is also merit in sometimes starting with our content. If we have just delivered great insights to one part of the company, are there now others that could benefit from the same content? The more time we spend cultivating knowledge about the big picture – how and why consumers in our market become customers of our organisation, and what our company should do differently to leverage the biggest opportunities and limit the largest risks – the more likely it is that we will produce a crop of insight that can be harvested again and again. This is especially true with senior audiences.

It is also possible to start with our communication channels. If we have opened up a new channel of communication to share one piece of content with one audience, let's consider how else we could now use that channel. At Barclays we hijacked the video screens in the elevators that took managers up to the top floors of our Canary Wharf head office. We initially just used them to show interviews with customers talking about topical issues but, having established the benefits of communicating to a captive audience, we then developed other content that would work through that channel. In turn, this focus on animated content led to a search for more channels through which we could show it, and so we came to use the large TV monitors in staff restaurants and on the walls of our call centres. 'Insight TV' became a whole programme of activity for us. But of course it wasn't suitable for all content, and nor could we use it to reach all audiences.

An Insight CMO should also consider things like a consistent tone of voice, a standard look and feel to documents, common use of language, and key messages that should be reinforced at every opportunity. And we also need to consider communication standards. We live in a world where the basic standard of most communications has improved dramatically over the last decade, either through sophisticated animation, more professional infographics or presentations, or a heightened awareness of language and how to use it to nudge the reader. In one respect this is great, because it means that Insight teams are likely to have a greater choice of communication methods at their disposal. But it has also raised the stakes: our corporate decision-makers are constantly bombarded with messages, many of them beautifully packaged, so if we expect our messages to gain cut through and become memorable we have to raise our game and put a lot more time and effort into the way we plan our Insight communication programme.

....

The 17th secret of successful Insight teams is that they drive change by designing and delivering an Insight communication programme

If you would like to explore this topic further, you might like to read the IMA's Insight leader guide *IMP402: How to plan an Insight communication programme*

....

Key points to consider:

1. Insight teams often work close to marketing departments but forget to market their own insights
2. To drive change we should plan an Insight communication programme and improve our communication standards
3. Most communication plans start with a focus on our audiences and consider the insight that would help them in their jobs
4. Sometimes we might start with the insight we already have – our content – and then look for new audiences for it
5. We can also review our communication channels and package our content in a way that would work through that channel

We can learn a lot if we step into the shoes of an Insight CMO, but we also need to think about the structure of the material we are going to communicate. So in the next chapter we're going to spend time with a friend we already met in chapter 5: the Insight consultant.

Chapter 18
Developing Insight stories

Back in 1987, Barbara Minto of McKinsey's wrote a book called *The Pyramid Principle* in which she recommended that all management consultants should structure their work using the SCQA framework. The letters stood for Situation, Complication, Question and Answer. Minto subsequently taught many of the major consultancy firms in North America and Europe to use this framework, advocating its benefits at two key phases: the project initiation phase, when consultants frame the issue they are going to investigate; and the recommendation phase, when conclusions and ideas are sold back to the client company.

The IMA launched the first Insight forum in London in early 2005, and one of its first best practice projects looked at the structure of Insight communications. The prevailing thinking up until then had been that analysis and research projects should be conducted and then written up as if they were scientific experiments. Market research reports in particular would start with a reference to the brief that had been received from the person commissioning the research; then go into detail about the methodology selected; the research activity carried out; the data collated and tables of findings. And finally, if you were lucky, some observations and conclusions.

This was a very logical way of approaching the task, but it's a very passive way of communicating. The Insight forum members thought it was particularly damaging for corporate Insight professionals because everything about it, from playing back the research brief to focusing on methodology, smacks of a reactive service provider employed largely for their technical expertise. It isn't consistent with a forward-looking Insight team that aspires to identify value for its business and drive change. A progressive Insight team wouldn't want to focus on research briefs but on the underlying business issue. Nor would they want to prioritise methodology when communicating to decision-makers; methodology is strictly an internal issue for the Insight team to sort out, and only merits a mention in an appendix when communicating to decision-makers.

The IMA's co-founder, Sally Webb immediately recognised the benefits available for corporate Insight teams if they adopted Barbara Minto's model. As we saw in chapter 5, we believe that it comes into its own right at the start of projects, helping Insight professionals to diagnose the real business issue to be investigated. But it is also our preferred way of structuring Insight communication at the end of projects, or, to be more precise, if you use this framework to develop your story throughout a piece of work, the structure of the communication is already there.

During the last 15 years we have made two alterations to the initial SCQA model. The first is to add a B at the end to highlight the Benefits of adopting the recommendations made. The second is to recognise that in practice it can be useful to identify more than one question to be addressed by Insight work, especially for analysts, albeit that there should be absolute clarity about the one key underlying business question. This is how the model works:

Situation: the background to the issue, big-picture stats about the existing state of the market or how customers interact with our organisation to create value.

Complication: the issue(s) that has arisen and caused the organisation to stop and think; this might be some adverse financial numbers, a change in the competitor landscape, or a perceived change in consumer behaviour.

Question: this is the key underlying business issue that this piece of Insight work addresses, expressed in a way which relates to possible actions for the company and to the potential financial impact. It frames everything that follows, with issues like methodology relegated to an appendix.

Answer: the message-led answer to the business issue summarised in the Question; this should be written in such a way that it can rolled up to a punchy headline, or rolled down to include more detail as appropriate for different audiences.

Benefit: the advantage of adopting the recommendation made in the Answer, ideally quantified in financial terms.

Many of the IMA's corporate members have now adopted SCQAB, and it has been among the top five requests for IMA training for over ten years. Some organisations, such as my former company Barclays, have thought it so central to Insight work that they have embedded the structure within their Insight communication templates. Not only has this helped them to communicate findings more effectively, it has also shaped their thinking throughout all the stages which led to the recommendations.

SCQAB also captures another truism about Insight communication: if you adopt this way of working, you will start to think about the communication of the story as you develop it. This underlines the point I made about Insight work being iterative in chapter 6:

- we constantly think about business issues
- we reflect on what we know already
- we identify hypotheses about why new things are happening or how a situation might develop
- we collect research and explore new data to substantiate or disprove our hypotheses
- we interpret the evidence we find, then amend our hypotheses

When Insight teams work in this way, the structure of our story evolves as we complete our investigation. It isn't something that we 'write up' at the end of our project, it's an integral part of the project itself. What we will still need to consider is the variety of methods we want to use to share our story, and some of these will require synthesis and succinct messages, others might need more detail. So there is definitely still a communication phase, one that might go on for many months after the investigation is complete if it's a message that lots of people need to hear. But the structure of the underlying story should be developed during the investigation, and the significant stats, logic and key phrases honed every time we repeat them.

....

The 18th secret of successful Insight teams is that they spend time optimising the structure of their Insight communications

If you would like to explore this topic further, you might like to read the IMA's Insight leader guide *IMP403: How to structure Insight communications*

....

Key points to consider:

1. The traditional way of writing up research projects reflects Insight teams' out-dated role as service providers

2. Barbara Minto's SCQ framework, as adapted by the IMA to SCQAB, provides a far punchier, message-led, issue-focused structure

3. SCQAB is very powerful at the start of projects, when Insight teams nail the business issue and diagnose the problem to be solved

4. SCQAB can then be used to shape our thinking so that the story evolves as the investigation progresses

5. SCQAB is consistent with a hypothesis-led, iterative way of thinking that reflects an internal business consultant role

This chapter has explored SCQAB and its role shaping Insight stories but there is more to storytelling than structure. In the next chapter we're going to meet three more professional communicators: the Insight author, the Insight journalist and the Insight editor.

Chapter 19
Sharing Insight stories

We all know that stories are powerful, probably the most widely used and effective communication tool in human history. They have helped whole societies to develop a narrative around how they came to exist and what they are striving to do, therefore forming an integral part of every culture. Big businesses have also used stories for years, narratives about their formation and evolution, and the role they play in satisfying consumer demand or wider society. Most of the adverts we see contain some form of storytelling, and there are stories in every sales pitch and new business proposal.

In recent years, organisations have woken up to the power of stories for internal communication, with CEOs investing a lot of time and budget developing a narrative and using compelling media to communicate their vision. So it is only natural that Insight teams have followed the same trend, and every research conference now includes at least one session on storytelling.

To meet this corporate demand, a lot of providers have started to advertise storytelling workshops, and many of them are very engaging. The problem is that most seem to be aimed at would-be novelists or film makers; they are far too conceptual for most analysts and researchers to find useful. The IMA often hears Insight leaders say that their Learning and Development department had arranged training on storytelling, but that it's now difficult to see how Insight team behaviour has changed as a result.

So, for our work on this topic, the IMA's Lisa Dutton has asked, 'What key principles emerge from the concept of storytelling, and how can we apply each back to our Insight work?'. To answer the question, we are going to look at three more characters: the Insight author, the Insight journalist, and the Insight editor:

Think like an author: let's start with our audience. In chapter 16 I suggested that our Insight teams should consider the audience for Insight communication programmes, but individual pieces of communication will have different audiences and it's never a bad idea to put ourselves in their shoes and consider what they most need to know.

Good books also have clear themes, both in terms of overall subjects – an aspect that should be guaranteed for us if we use an SCQAB structure anyway – but also angles on those subjects, or analogies, or rhetorical devices to which an author keeps returning to provide their story with rhythm and flow.

Another aspect advocated by many authors, but not all, is storyboarding: the importance of sketching out the way that the narrative will lead the reader through the scenes and arrive at a natural conclusion. A few years ago I was lucky enough to hear the celebrated author Robert Harris speak at the Warwick Words book festival, and he described how he had begun his first book, *Fatherland*, without a clear idea of where his story was going to go. He was pleased with the first few pages but arrived at the 35th page to find that he had all his leading characters gathered in the same room, and suddenly realised that he didn't know why they were there or what was going to happen next. At that point, he put his first draft to one side, and sketched out ideas for the rest of the book from beginning to end, and only when he was happy with the conclusion did he begin the process of revealing the story that he now knew.

There is much that Insight analysts and market researchers can learn from here. On the one hand it is imperative that we develop our overall project story as we go through each Insight investigation, but the actual writing of individual pieces of communication should be done once we know the conclusion we have reached and the key aspects to share so that our readers arrive at the same place.

Think like a journalist: and start with our headlines. Headline-writing has been elevated to an artform in journalism, with more time spent getting the half a dozen words in big bold print right than any other words in the story. It's the headline alone that grabs our attention and makes us click on one story for more information rather than another one. Not only do Insight teams need to think about titles for their reports, but the headlines for their conclusions and individual pages or slides. Choosing a passive headline that describes the data versus an active headline that conveys a punchy message can make all the difference to whether your audience engages with your story.

Headlines that make an impact are also more likely to leave an impression. Insight audiences – our key decision-makers, or the broader groups of colleagues who consume our content when we are not in the room – are not likely to be in a position to take action there and then. They will leave the presentation and go onto several other meetings or put down a report and answer a call. To be motivated to take action, or carry forward the key findings into a meeting later in the week when a related business issue is discussed, we need to find a form of words that will stick in their heads.

Another aspect of journalism that Insight professionals can all learn from is the importance of bringing stories to life by focusing on the specific human instance that illustrates the broader message being conveyed. Thousands of people killed in motor accidents is a statistic, but one mother grieving for a teenager knocked off a motorbike is a human tragedy. This is an area where market researchers and customer analysts can help each other: analysis, and quant research is great for producing the big numbers that show the scale of an issue and the importance of taking action; but qualitative research (or recordings from call centres, video vox pops, etc) are brilliant at bringing an individual customer into the story.

Think like an editor: last but not least, good communication requires good editing, because most of what we put in our first draft deserves to be discarded.

Editors help to keep pieces of communication simple and focussed, so we should always ask others to go through our work before publishing it. As I know to my own cost, we are all poor editors of our own writing!

A key take out for Insight teams is to allow time to edit. That might seem obvious, but in a world where there is always pressure for talented analysts and researchers to move onto the next investigation, it's tempting to breathe a sigh of relief when we have finished writing our reports, building our presentations or compiling our videos. It can make an enormous difference if we allow ourselves time to rehearse, prune and polish, or give a colleague time to read, reflect and edit our work.

....

The 19th secret of successful Insight teams is that they develop their storytelling skills to help them to drive change

If you would like to explore this topic further, you might like to read the IMA's Insight leader guide *IMP404: Storytelling for Insight teams*

....

Key points to consider:

1. Stories are powerful, probably the most widely used and effective communication tool in human history
2. Many organisations arrange storytelling training, but then discover that it is difficult to apply the high-minded principles to Insight work
3. We should learn from how authors tell stories to a chosen audience and improve the flow of the narrative and with storyboarding
4. We can also learn from journalists, and their expertise in crafting headlines that make an impact and leave an impression
5. We must always allow time to edit, and ask our colleagues to review our work and sharpen our stories

We have now met five of the six characters of Insight communication. In the next chapter, the last one in this section on *Driving Change*, we're going to meet the final character: the Insight designer.

Chapter 20
Painting Insight pictures

Napoleon Bonaparte said that 'a good sketch is better than a long speech', and increasingly organisations are using visual communication to get their messages across to customers.

As consumers ourselves, we recognise that images are often easier to follow than words: from the ubiquitous IKEA self-assembly instructions, to the colourful infographics in the Sunday newspapers, and the YouTube video guides on how to manage every aspect of our lives. Internal corporate departments have tended to be slower to use visual communications but, done well, they can be an extremely effective tool for an Insight team. Done badly, they can over-complicate and confuse.

Why are visuals important?

- We are 'visually wired': scientists believe that 50% of our brain is involved in visual processing, and we can get the sense of a visual scene in less than one-tenth of a second.

- We find visuals more engaging: research shows that colourful visuals increase a willingness to read by 80%.

- We also find visual communications more accessible: a study of comprehension rates of medicine labels showed 70% for labels with text only, versus 95% with text and pictures. And people following directions with text and illustrations do more than three times better than people following directions without illustrations (as demonstrated by those IKEA instructions).

- Finally, we find visual communication more persuasive: one study showed that 50% of an audience was persuaded by a purely verbal presentation, versus 67% of the audience who were persuaded by the verbal presentation plus accompanying visuals. Simply adding pictures of brain scans and mentioning cognitive neuroscience makes people more inclined to believe what they are reading!

The complication is that as Insight professionals we are not artists nor graphic designers, and we wouldn't have the time to spend hours creating masterpieces even if we were. So, how can we make our visual communications look good and have impact? The answer is threefold:

First we can train ourselves to think like an Insight designer and give some thought to how we can solve problems and present ideas visually. It doesn't have to be complicated; we can have huge impact just by using simple shapes like triangles, squares and circles to communicate our ideas. Kevin Duncan's *The Diagrams Book* is a great source of inspiration and he demonstrates how very simple shapes can be used to great effect. Some good examples include:

(a) A pyramid with three bands, where the base often illustrates a platform, a middle band is a transition area, and the peak an achievement, a destination or an elite group. The pyramid is very useful for Insight teams when describing the shape of their organisation's customer base, or the market within which it operates: typically, high volume or mass market at the base, with lower volume but higher value (or profitability, or engagement) towards the top.

(b) Squares and 4-box models: one axis can express time or direction, a second creates a grid and if you enclose it you've got the consultant's beloved 4-box model. One famous example of this is the priority matrix found in Stephen Covey's *The Seven Habits of Highly Effective People*, another is Ansoff's Matrix (the new product / market expansion grid).

(c) Venn diagrams: provide a highly flexible system of interlocking circles with many applications for Insight teams. You can use circles to represent different customer groups defined by product holdings, needs or demographics. How the circles overlap demonstrates groups with shared characteristics and areas of uniqueness, and circle size can be varied to represent volume.

Further examples found in Kevin Duncan's book are the rising wedge, the whittling wedge, the target and the cycle.

Second, we can marry the talents of the Insight designer to those of the Insight editor and produce charts that enable one key message to stand out. David McCandless, data journalist and author of *Information is beautiful*, believes that all Insight professionals have a 'dormant design literacy' that gives us the potential to produce effective infographics; Cole Nussbaumer Knaflic of Storytelling with Data has effectively demonstrated the power of decluttering our charts in her YouTube videos.

Finally, moving images are even more compelling than still images, and we should look for ways to incorporate animations and video footage of consumers at every opportunity. The late Hans Rosling, author of *Factfulness*, was celebrated for his moving bubble charts (see examples on YouTube) and many progressive Insight teams from Unilever to CocaCola make great use of customer vox pops on their Insight portals. Diane Earnshaw, founder of Vox Pops International, was a leading pioneer of the use of videos in Insight communications and her company has now developed ways of animating spreadsheets and dashboards to make them more engaging and allow Insight teams to overlay context and recommendations.

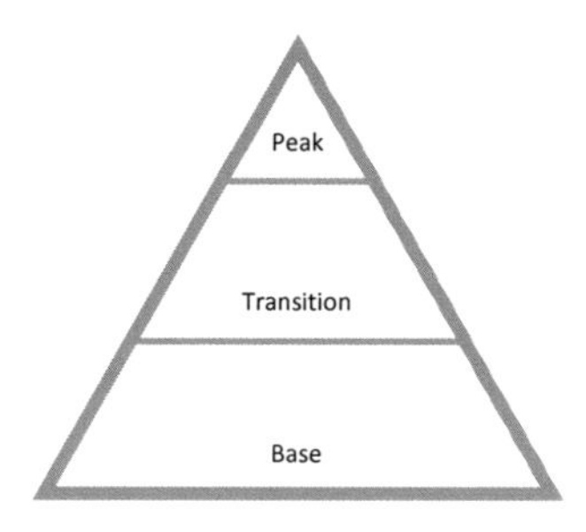

Figure 1: Pyramid

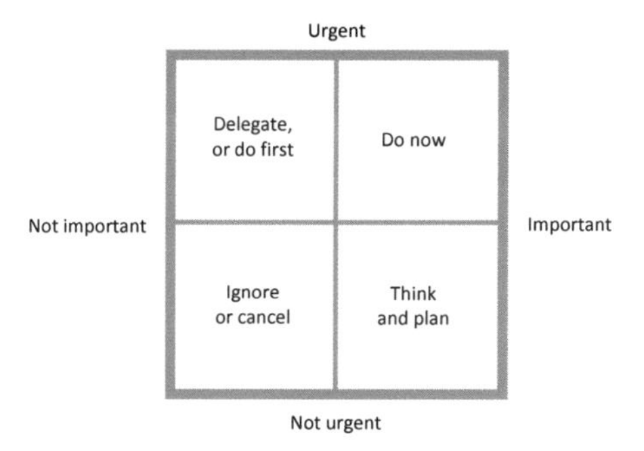

Figure 2: Priority matrix

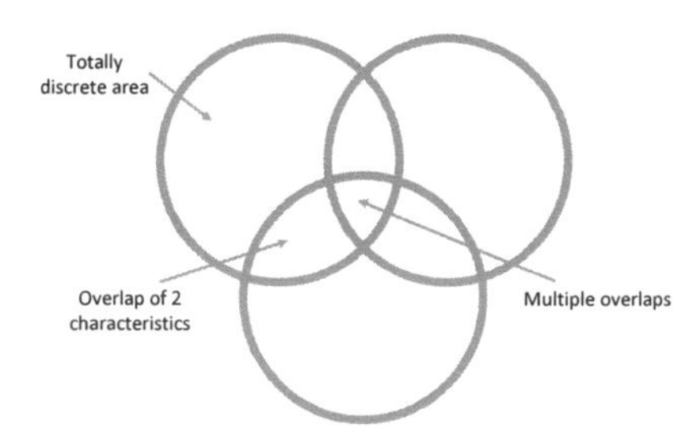

Figure 3: Venn diagram

....

The 20th secret of successful Insight teams is that they develop their visual communication skills to tell stories through pictures and diagrams

If you would like to explore this topic further, you might like to read the IMA's Insight leader guide *IMP405: Visual communication for Insight teams*

....

Key points to consider:

1. A good sketch is usually better than a long speech; we are hard-wired to take more notice of colourful pictures than of boring text
2. Our brains not only take more notice of visual communications, they find them more engaging, accessible and persuasive
3. Insight professionals are not usually design specialists but we can all learn to illustrate our ideas with simple diagrams
4. We should also edit our charts, decluttering standard templates so that a clear message stands out
5. Moving images are even more compelling so we should find ways to incorporate animations and video footage of consumers

This completes our ten chapters on *Driving Change*, but there is still much to consider if you want to transform your Insight team. Everything that we have looked at so far relates to Insight team activity and will enable a real evolution in your team's effectiveness. But what happens if you need a revolution? It's now time to really focus on our roles as Insight leaders, and this is going to require a new, top-down perspective.

Section 3

Leading Insight strategy and people

Leading Insight strategy and people

In the third section of *Transforming Insight*, we will focus on the next ten secrets of successful corporate Insight teams:

Chapter 21
A strategy for Insight

In the first two sections of *Transforming Insight* we've explored the purpose of Insight teams and the four principal activities on which team members should focus. If you work in a corporate Insight team and you take a progressive approach to generating new insights, farming customer knowledge, influencing key decision-makers and communicating understanding, then you will certainly identify more value for your organisation and drive more change within it.

But throughout this book I have referred to *Insight leaders* – the senior professionals who run the Insight departments in large companies, or the senior managers who might be responsible for Insight and other functions in smaller organisations. If that's you, then I have a challenge for you: is it enough to do things better? Will rebalancing your resources between these four principal activities ensure that your CEO gets maximum value for money from his or her investment in Insight? Will it, over time, create an Insight-driven organisation?

Customer and Market Insight has the potential to transform an organisation's performance. It can identify hidden opportunities in the market, and increase a company's sales, customer growth and revenue far above the level it would otherwise achieve. It can also shine a light on potential threats, define tangible responses to them, and so help to safeguard an organisation's very existence.

Spending on research and analysis tends to be small in relation to overall revenue and costs, so Insight is capable of generating an enormous financial return on investment for an organisation. In a large company that can mean spending thousands to generate millions. Seen through this lens, Insight, as a concept and as a corporate department, should be regarded as a key strategic asset for an organisation, whether it operates in the commercial sector, the not-for-profit sector, or the public sector.

But is that how it feels in your organisation? This sort of impact is only possible if Insight is set up to do the right things as well as do things right. And it needs the right operating environment and resources if it's going to consistently drive change across the whole organisation.

What is actually happening?

Demand for insights within organisations is rising as senior management increasingly acknowledges the importance of customer-centricity and see research and analytics as a potential source of competitive advantage. At the same time, the proliferation of digital transactions and data sources has increased the complexity of managing Insight activity. As a result, many Insight functions report an ever-growing workload, with less time to stop and think about big questions, like why your organisation has an Insight team, how much it spends on Insight activity, what return it gets on its investment, and whether there are structural issues to challenge if you want to create an Insight-driven organisation.

As the potential for Insight to make a difference increases, and as the difficulties in making it make a difference rise, there is a critical need for organisations to define their strategy for Insight. This is very different from an activity plan; every research and analytics team has one of those! This is a top down assessment of how your company's performance could be improved with the systematic application of customer and market understanding, and what changes would have to be brought about to make that happen

The challenges of developing an Insight strategy

Despite the apparent need for an Insight strategy, the IMA's research with members in the UK, North America and Europe has found that less than a quarter of large organisations have written one. Why is this? Do Insight leaders not see the need for an Insight strategy? Or is the problem that we lack the confidence to write one? Or is it that we might like to develop one, and maybe feel we should, but other things get in the way?

From our research, and from the client-side experience of our consultants, it would appear that the main barriers are:

- Not knowing where to start
- Being too busy to spend time writing it
- Being put off by the word 'strategy'
- Having a service mentality and not seeing the need for it
- The pace of organisational change risks invalidating it
- Organisational culture doesn't value strategies

Taking these challenges together, there is a widespread belief that developing an Insight strategy is a difficult thing to do, and that the benefits of having one would not outweigh the pain of producing it. But in the absence of an Insight strategy, research and analysis activity tends to be driven by what other departments want. A strategy in itself may not change that, of course, but it is a critical place to start.

Isn't it enough to have an Insight plan? Many Insight leaders will produce and update an Insight plan, but in many cases these documents (or spreadsheets) simply record the requests received or Insight projects to which resource has been allocated. They are very important documents, and no Insight team could survive without them. But they are not designed to transform Insight's contribution to the organisation, let alone describe how Insight might transform the organisation's performance.

The IMA believes that Insight leaders need to move their planning upstream, ideally developing a strategic plan for Insight which either aligns directly with a top-level corporate strategy, or better still, examines the data and thinking behind that corporate strategy.

Armed with a truly strategic plan for how Insight can make a difference, Insight leaders can then identify priority questions to address with existing customer and market knowledge, or gaps to plug with new market research and analysis. We must engage our key stakeholders at every step, because there is no point Insight pursuing an agenda which leads to output that the rest of the business will ignore. But what is needed is grown-up discussion about existing customer knowledge and new work which could be undertaken, not an order-taking mentality where new research or analysis is commissioned without reference to a top-down Insight plan.

Developing an Insight strategy need not be a difficult thing to do, but it does take a disciplined approach, time and focus.

....

The 21st secret of successful Insight teams is that they lead the development of an Insight strategy for their organisation

If you would like to explore this topic further, you might like to read the IMA's Insight leader guide *IMP501: An introduction to Insight strategy*

....

Key points to consider:

1. Taking a progressive approach to Insight generation, knowledge, influence and communication is critical, but not enough
2. If we want Insight to transform our organisation's performance, then we need to take a more strategic approach to transforming Insight
3. In the absence of a strategy, most Insight teams have an activity plan, but very often this is driven purely by what other departments want
4. Insight leaders need to get upstream, to align Insight to, and be prepared to challenge, corporate strategy at the highest level
5. Developing an Insight strategy is not necessarily that difficult, but it does need a disciplined approach, time and focus

So if we're going to write a strategy, what should it include? Well, we'll clearly need a vision of where we would like to get to, the options for how we could get there, and an execution plan for us to make it happen. But before we can take decisions about any of those things, it's going to need something that we should all be good at: some analysis and reflection. That's what we'll look at in the next chapter.

Chapter 22
The opportunity to make a difference

Imagine that it's your first day as Insight Director at a company you haven't worked for before. Maybe it's a sector that you don't know at all. It's a completely fresh start. After your initial induction meetings, you meet the CEO or Managing Director. Probably not your immediate boss, but the person your boss reports to.

The CEO cuts straight to the point. She's been reading in the *Harvard Business Review* that the most progressive companies believe that Insight has the power to transform an organisation's performance. However, her experience of Insight in this organisation has been quite different. She doesn't really know the team very well but understands that it is a function respected for its technical analysis skills and its grasp of market research methodologies; but it's not really a group who play a leading role driving the performance of the overall company. There's nothing wrong with the people, it's just that this isn't the role that Insight has played here, nor the role which senior managers have expected it to play.

So her challenge to you is simple: come back in 90 days and tell me exactly what we need to do to make Insight make a real difference here. What's your vision for Insight?

It's not just new Insight leaders who are asked to explain their vision for the future of course, You can design a new vision for Insight in your organisation at any time, and you don't need to wait to be asked. However, there is something about the mindset of a newly appointed leader that makes it a particularly easy time to think about things clearly, so if you have been in your role, company or sector for some time, it might help to imagine that you are new to your role. At the 54th meeting of the IMA's Insight forum in London in September 2018, we gave all the representatives a new job for the afternoon to reinforce this point.

Some people love thinking about their vision for the future of Insight. Others are filled with dread. So where would you start? The top tips from IMA members are:

- Give yourself the time and space to reflect properly, in a structured way
- Have the courage to think big, because ideas will always be scaled back

If this seems like a weighty responsibility, the good news is that the first phase is not to conjure up a brilliant form of words that can immediately satisfy your CEO and motivate your colleagues. First you need to do some analysis to make sure that you really understand the lie of the land. Only once we have made an assessment of the ways in which Insight could make a difference, can we reflect on our ambition for Insight to actually make that difference in our organisation.

Understanding the lie of the land

We are going to explore this in six steps. The first two steps might surprise you because they do not relate to the Insight function at all but rather to understanding the market in which your company operates, and your organisation within that market.

- The best place to start your analysis, is to look beyond your organisation altogether, to look out of the window and focus on real people living their lives. Which aspect of their life is your organisation trying to improve? Which market is your company really in? Is that market static, changing, growing or disappearing?

- We can then look at how our organisations are succeeding or failing in their market. How do they interact with customers and is this interaction successful? Does it create value for the consumer, and value for the company? What challenges and opportunities does it face if it wants to improve its performance?

The next steps relate to a different market – the internal market for Insight within your company:

- First we need to understand corporate assumptions: an Insight team doesn't function in a vacuum, but rather in an environment made up of many other departments and their senior leaders. Individually these teams are likely to have a distinct mindset, with specific managers having a focus that is partly driven by the corporate seat they sit in, and partly by their own personalities and experiences. But it is also likely that your organisation has a collective mindset, a group of assumptions about how things are done, what needs to be worried about, and what it is safe to ignore.

- The next step is to consider the way that your CEO and senior management team make decisions, because it's only by influencing those decisions that the Insight team can make a difference. There is a parallel here with Insight teams wanting to understand what exactly drives consumers' decisions, and, just as with consumers, it is very likely that you will find some claimed assertions about how decisions are taken (for example, formal committee structures) plus an awareness that there may be some deeper reasons, driven by behavioural biases, that are more difficult to uncover.

Only then should you look at your current Insight capability and knowledge, and the extent to which they are fit for purpose if you want to transform company performance.

- We'll start with an audit of your organisation's current Insight capability. Which things does it do well? Where is it best in class? Where is it behind other companies? If you are not sure, the IMA has a suite of benchmarking tools that are tailor-made to support leaders with this, including a 10-minute *Transforming Insight* survey that is available free to all members.

- Finally, it is also important to assess your company's current 'knowledge asset'. What does it know about its markets, its customers, their interactions with the organisation, and how value is created for both the consumer and the company? Customer knowledge tends to be patchy within most organisations, with various versions of the truth existing in different places, and different levels of reliance placed on the same evidence. This is not surprising: most companies either have a fragmented approach to generating new insights in the first place, or they focus their Insight activity predominantly on finding out new things, not on working out how all the things they have already discovered relate to each other.

Once you have gathered evidence in each of these six steps, it's time to join the dots and reflect on what success could look like for your company, what role Insight could play in this, and how well equipped it is to play that role at the moment.

....

The 22nd secret of successful Insight teams is that they survey the lie of the land to understand the opportunity for Insight

If you would like to explore this topic further, you might like to read the IMA's Insight leader guide *IMP502: How to understand the lie of the land*

....

Key points to consider:

1. You can design a new vision for Insight in your organisation at any time, you don't need to wait to be asked
2. There is something about being new to a role, a company or a sector that makes it easier however, so grab these opportunities
3. To understand the opportunity for Insight, first think about your external market and your organisation's place within it
4. Then consider the internal market for Insight: your company's current plans and the way it goes about making decisions
5. Finally look at your current Insight capability and knowledge: are they fit for purpose if you want transform company performance?

It's tempting to start drawing conclusions at this stage and begin writing a new vision for Insight. But before you get too far with that, I'd like you to reflect on one more question: what is your real ambition for Insight? That's not a question we consider very often, so that's what we'll explore in the next chapter.

Chapter 23
Defining your ambition

As we saw in the last chapter, understanding the lie of the land is a critical part of the strategy development process, but it doesn't in itself define a vision for where Insight might get to. Creating a successful vision for your Insight function can only be achieved by examining both the potential ways for Insight to make a difference to your organisation's performance and your ambition for it to actually seize those opportunities.

Ambition is not a subject often discussed in Insight circles. Of course individual members of teams might be recognised as ambitious, and I'm sure you have conversations with your colleagues about their ambitions in 121s and personal development sessions. But what is your ambition for Insight as a function and a concept in your company? How much does your own personal ambition cause you to be optimistic about how transformative a role Insight could play? Or does your lack of career ambition - maybe for very good reasons - impede your thinking when you consider the potential for Insight?

The leader responsible for Insight at one of the global retailers who work most closely with the IMA believes that there is a very strong connection between an Insight leader's personal ambition and the vision which they define for Insight in their company. This can work both ways: ambitious individuals can encourage their teams to reach for the stars before they are ready to fly; equally, more cautious Insight leaders can fail to recognise their team's true potential because they may not be interested in further promotion for themselves.

So, for this part of the strategy development process, I'd like you to consider:

- Your ambition as an Insight leader
- Your ambition for your team
- Your ambition for Insight to become a key part of your company
- Your ambition for your organisation itself

Something else that might influence your thinking in this space is the ambition shown by other Insight leaders. Whether you meet your peers at one of the IMA's Insight forums, through professional associations, research and analysis conferences or online networking groups, it is worth reflecting on the ambition that they reveal when they talk about Insight's role in their organisation. Very often we assume that other Insight leaders share our perspective, but listen carefully to what research and analysis directors say, and it is usually possible to divine something about their ambition – or lack of ambition - for their function.

A final thing to consider, and this is a little more difficult to define, revolves around a combination of leaders' (and their team's):

- sense of mission
- tradition
- values
- culture
- desired impact

Collectively this might be described as 'the way we want to play the game'. Or to adopt the language you would expect to read in a chapter about strategy, 'how would we like Insight to participate in the life of the wider organisation?' One way to consider this is through the lens of the IMA's Insight participation matrix:

Figure 4: Insight team participation matrix

Service delivery: If an Insight team focuses primarily on contributing analysis and research to individual projects, and the research or analysis is mainly concerned with what is happening, where, when, by whom, and why, it is likely to be playing the role of a service delivery function. This is where most Insight teams have traditionally played, and it can be a very comfortable place to be. But it is not going to transform your organisation's performance.

Voice of the customer: Moving up to the top left quadrant of the matrix, we can identify a role that many Insight teams now aspire to play, particularly if they have a market research heritage. To become the *voice of the customer* (VoC), they need to combine project delivery with an increasing focus on joining the dots between projects, and forming opinions based on the joined-up evidence. However, the IMA does not regard this as the optimal role for an Insight team to play. Business decisions always involve trade-offs, and if the Insight team is merely amplifying views expressed in customer research, it is leaving it to others to work out how to make the trade-off between customer, financial and operational factors. It is not really mapping from the market to the money.

Project consultants: Insight leaders who would like their functions to move out of the bottom-left service delivery quadrant can also be drawn to the bottom right quadrant. This we have labelled *project consultancy* and it is the polar opposite of the voice of the customer positioning. This project consultant role is being increasingly adopted by more progressive analysis-based teams and its focus on objectively analysing all data (customer, market, operational, financial, etc) relevant to a particular decision gives it much in common with management consultancy. Unlike the VoC role above it does involve mapping from the market to the money, but an Insight team working in this way ignores another crucial part of its remit: to develop a customer knowledge asset and a coherent set of opinions about the direction of the whole business, not just the specific business issue being debated.

Strategy drivers: The top right quadrant is occupied by those Insight teams who try to combine the big picture opinions of the voice of the customer teams, with the solution-focused contribution of the project consultants. We have labelled these teams *strategy drivers* to recognise that they have developed an opinion about how and why consumers in a market become customers of an organisation and create value for it.

If you read the first section of this book and thought 'I want my team to farm Insight knowledge' and also 'I want us to map right from the market to the money'; then you went onto the second section and you thought 'there is no point doing either of those things unless we drive change through influence and communication' then this is a natural place for you to want to play. But be under no illusion: combining all these aspirations can produce the ultimate ambition for Insight, but are you prepared to take on that challenge?

....

The 23rd secret of successful Insight teams is that they identify their ambition for Insight in their organisation

If you would like to explore this topic further, you might like to read the IMA's Insight leader guide *IMP503: Defining your ambition for Insight*

....

Key points to consider:

1. To create a vision you need to understand the opportunities to make a difference and your ambition to seize those opportunities
2. The ambition shown by an Insight team often reflects the ambition of its leader, so consider the difference between the two
3. The Insight team participation matrix provides a lens through which we can examine our ambition for Insight
4. Progressive Insight teams are moving away from service delivery to become the voice of the customer or project consultants
5. The IMA believes that the ultimate ambition for an Insight team is to be strategy drivers, combining the best of all the other roles

You should now be able to develop a vision for Insight based on your analysis of the lie of the land and your reflection on team ambition. Often that seems to be as far Insight leaders get, but if we want our strategy to be more than words on a page we now need to think through some practical implications. This is what we'll do in the next chapter.

Chapter 24
Identifying options

An important aspect of any strategy development is the need to move from relatively high-level statements about vision to some practical decisions about what is actually going to happen next.

The classic next step for many leaders is to talk to their teams. If you are an extrovert or naturally inclusive in the way that you make decisions, then you may have discussed your thinking about the opportunities and ambition for Insight before you came to any conclusions about your vision. But not everyone will have done this: you might be an introvert, or have good reasons for not being too inclusive too early - for example if you sense that radical change is going to be necessary and it would be inappropriate to discuss the direction of travel with your team before you have agreed the basics with your boss.

Many IMA members have found that an excellent way to engage their team is to talk to them about the vision they have developed, then invite either their whole team, a senior group, or a working party, to set about crafting a mission statement. In fact it's also not uncommon for Insight leaders to start with this step and miss out the analysis and vision stages, and I guess it's better to have a mission statement than nothing else; but I hope that the previous two chapters have demonstrated why there's a lot of profound thinking that should really happen first.

For Insight teams, a mission statement usually takes the essence of a vision, and crafts it into a punchy sentence that describes what the team aims to do and what effect this will have. A good mission statement can be really motivational, and it can also act as a reference point when deciding what a team will do during the year – and just as importantly, what it will not do. Some mission statement developed in recent years by IMA members include:

Aviva: To be laser-focussed on delivering what the business needs now and for tomorrow to deliver profitable game-changing Customer First propositions and communications

Lucozade Ribena Suntory: Inspire game-changing marketing and innovation

Dixons Carphone: To help the business to make customer informed decisions which make or save money

British Gas: Driving customer centricity through informing and driving decision making

Spire Healthcare: To be the people who enable better decision making leading to fundamental business growth

Domestic & General: Insight exists to give the organisation the ability to make informed decisions, and to challenge the business

Abcam: To be catalysts for growth across the business through Anticipation, Automation and Advancing Scientific experiences

First Rate Exchange Services: To contribute to organisational and commercial success by engaging the business with insight, optimising decision making and proactively identifying opportunities

NFU Mutual: To provide clear pictures of what our existing and potential customers think, feel and do today and into the future, identifying value for the business and informing the interactions we need to have

Leonard Cheshire Disability: To influence decision-making and actions, to enable LCD to significantly increase our influence, reach and impact, broadening opportunities for people living with disability, everywhere

Mission statements like these can play an important first step in turning a vision into reality, but only the first step. Like any other corporate department, an Insight team will operate within certain parameters, carrying out work of a certain type, within a certain budget, and producing a range of outputs. These parameters should be the result of conscious choices evaluated in a written strategy.

However, only one in six Insight leaders say that their organisation always makes explicit choices about the Insight team's scope, scale, activity and output. Insight teams tend to carry on doing what they have done before. They often do not review from first principles what choices could be made and judge which options they should take. Instead, new choices are often forced upon Insight teams when they have to take on additional work or cut back on their budget or headcount.

The most effective Insight leaders take a proactive view of these issues and make recommendations about them which are consistent with their vision of the future. It is very important that this is written down, because putting it in writing forces leaders to confront trade-offs and issues which can otherwise be brushed aside.

Here are some key aspects for you to consider:

- **Scale of decisions to be influenced:** for some IMA members these are global, for others they relate only to one city; they might relate to every service your company provides through every channel, or be limited to one brand and product

- **Scope of Insight function:** is yours the only Insight team? Are there others providing analysis, research, competitor intelligence, management information, etc. Why are the parameters set where they are?

- **Type of activity:** this is the continuum from data sourcing, structuring and manipulation through to interpretation, communication and action-planning. Where does your work start and where does it end?

- **Output from the team:** is this data, information, real insights, or opinions and recommendations? Do you package it in reports, presentations, fact-packs, intranet portals or a wider range of communication devices?

- **Resources needed to fulfil this:** How big is your team? What skills does it include? How big is your budget? What discretion do you have about how it is spent?

- **Relationships with other departments:** Do they see you as a service function or trusted adviser? Do you rely on others for data or procuring research? Do you compete with others for providing opinions and recommendations?

- **Measures of success:** At the end of the year, how will you be judged? Is there alignment between your vision for Insight and the topics that will come up in your own annual review?

Just like the process of developing a vision, it is important to think creatively and think big because if you constrain your thinking at this stage then there's every chance that you will actually implement something even less ambitious. But the options and recommendations we make also have to be practical, because this is the point in the strategy development process when we move from big aspirations to specific, tangible issues. So we should include a view of key assumptions, risks and dependencies.

....

The 24th secret of successful Insight teams is that they take their vision for Insight and translate it into options for how they should operate

If you would like to explore this topic further, you might like to read the IMA's Insight leader guide *IMP504: How to identify options for your Insight team*

....

Key points to consider:

1. There is no point developing a vision for Insight and then leaving it as words on a page
2. Many leaders engage their team in crafting mission statements to provide them with motivation and a shared reference point
3. It is important to examine the parameters within which your Insight team is working and decide how they align to your vision
4. Key questions relate to the scale and scope of Insight activity, your resources and the way you work with other departments
5. Take nothing for granted: this could be your opportunity to enact real change, but consider the practical implications and trade offs

You will put yourself in a great position if you can produce a written document that not only captures your vision for Insight and the reasoning behind it, but also critiques the implications of that vision on how your department should operate going forward. But even a comprehensive strategy like this still needs to be executed, so that is what we'll consider in the next chapter.

Chapter 25
Executing strategy

You can formulate the most brilliant strategy, but if you cannot execute it, you might as well not have bothered. Execution is where many strategies go awry, and business schools tell us that this creates a performance gap between their planned and actual impact. The *Harvard Business Review* estimates that companies typically lose between 40% and 60% of their strategic potential during the execution phase. The same is likely to be true for an Insight strategy.

If we aspire to run an effective Insight team then we need to have a well-prepared plan for executing our Insight strategy and give proper thought and focus to the challenges we will face as we try to implement it. However, of the 200 organisations that the IMA has benchmarked in the last three years, only one in ten Insight leaders have said that they think they really manage their time in such a way that they can focus on implementing their organisation's Insight strategy.

Organisational change

Strategy execution is essentially an exercise in organisational change, involving, amongst other things, an understanding of the barriers to change and ways of overcoming them. However, as Insight leaders we tend not to be experts in organisational change; it's quite likely that we might have a technical background in market research or analysis and be quite inexperienced in implementing strategy. If this is the first Insight strategy we have written, we may feel that the hard work is done when we have crafted our vision and come up with some profound recommendations for what our departments should do differently in future. We might not appreciate the resistance we will face in actually making these changes happen.

Research by the Gartner Group has suggested that the number one reason for a change initiative to fail is the inability of people to alter their behaviour, skills and commitment to the new requirements. Major change only takes place successfully when people shift their values, aspirations, skills and behaviours. Effective change management overcomes resistance and builds the necessary commitment in people which then enables them to be ready, willing and able to change.

Every change project will have its supporters and detractors, both within and outside the Insight team. Identifying barriers to change and options for overcoming them always takes time and effort. As for any transformation programme, this part of the strategy needs to consider the best practice principles for change management. These include identifying and classifying key stakeholders according to the extent to which they currently buy into the need for change. This analysis will then determine how you involve them and communicate to them going forwards.

Effective Insight leaders set out a detailed and realistic plan to implement their Insight strategy which breaks down what needs to be done into steps – maybe over a period of up to three years. It is generally not realistic to achieve major change in Insight capability in a large organisation in a shorter timeframe, whilst a longer timeframe feels too distant and is too likely to be hijacked by other organisational changes.

Our plan should include quick wins and short-term milestones as well as our long-term objectives. Making a noticeable difference relatively early on signals change and success wins support for further change.

This sort of change programme also needs mechanisms built in to provide support and challenge during the change. For instance, it might require some temporary help to project manage the change programme itself and some external best practice expertise to provide an independent perspective on progress.

We also need to consider the various groups of people whose active or tacit support we are going to need, and to segment people in each group into likely evangelists, passive supporters, potential grumblers and possible terrorists. Include:

- **Your immediate boss:** some Insight leaders will have a very hands-on, supportive line manager and they will have discussed the Insight strategy with them at every step. This might include the analysis of the lie of the land, their reflections on an ambition and vision for Insight, and the whole set of key questions that we identified in chapter 24. If your strategy recommends large changes to team structure, budget, activity and measures of success then you will clearly need your line manager's active support.

- **More senior executives:** these can range from your boss's boss, to the directors of other departments that have a reliance on or influence over Insight activity, like marketing, finance, corporate strategy or product management. Who could help you to execute your strategy, or has the potential to veto parts of it?

- **Your existing Insight team:** your strategy might have profound implications for some of the people who already work in Insight, possibly including job losses or major role changes. When you look across the desk, which colleagues will be your natural supporters, and which will only see the problems rather than the opportunities?

- **The wider Insight community:** depending on the changes you advocate, there might be people in other departments whose roles are brought into Insight, or departments whose work is affected by

> what the Insight team start or stop doing. It can be easy to forget colleagues in parallel divisions who may be uncomfortable with what you propose and become entrenched opponents of your new way of working.

The precise circumstances you face, the pace of change you desire, the barriers to progress that you will meet will all differ enormously by company. Only you can reflect on the universe that you need to win over and the milestones you need to achieve along the way.

....

The 25th secret of successful Insight teams is that they devote time and effort to executing their Insight strategy

If you would like to explore this topic further, you might like to read the IMA's Insight leader guide *IMP505: How to execute your Insight strategy*

....

Key points to consider:

1. Most strategies go wrong at the implementation stage

2. Insight strategy execution is an exercise in organisation change so it needs to be thought about as a separate step

3. Map the journey that you hope to take and identify key milestones, dependencies and measures of success

4. The support you receive from your boss and other senior executives will be critical to making big changes happen

5. You will also need support from key colleagues in and around the Insight department so remember not to take them for granted

As we have explored the ways to develop an Insight strategy, the more it has become apparent that we are reliant on our Insight people. In fact, managing and developing our Insight colleagues is a vital part of every Insight leader's role. So in the next five chapters I am going to move on from our role leading Insight strategy to look at the next topic: leading Insight people.

Chapter 26
It's all about the people

Many years ago I had to sit through the most excruciating leaving speech I've ever heard. The man who was leaving was a big boss, an exceptionally capable business leader but a guy who could be a real monster to work for. He routinely sacrificed his junior colleagues' happiness, work-life balance and sense of self-worth to the greater glory of his own ambition, and the entire business division which he led was extremely relieved when he announced that he was leaving. But in his speech on the last day, he astounded everyone by declaring how much he would miss us… 'because at the end of the day, it's all about the people, isn't it?'

On that day, many years ago, there was an awkward silence before we remembered that we were supposed to supply some polite applause. But that closing phrase has often come back to me over the years, because, when it comes to developing an effective Insight team, it really is all about the people.

Developing effective Insight teams

As Insight leaders we all really want to develop the most effective Insight function we can, and in this book I've already covered lots of ways of doing that:

- The importance of defining insights and insight, and appreciating that the true purpose of an Insight team is to identify value for our organisations and to drive change within them

- The many ways we can improve our departments' ability to identify value through generating new insights and also by farming customer knowledge

- The mindset and behaviour necessary to drive change through influence and communication

- The responsibility which all Insight leaders share for identifying a strategy for Insight, including a vision showing the difference Insight could make in our particular companies

However, a focus on what our departments do and which processes they follow is no substitute for thinking about our people, their skills, and how we deploy them. In chapter 21 I said that fewer than one in every six large organisations has an Insight strategy; but the IMA's benchmarking work has shown that even fewer have a structured plan for thinking about their Insight people.

This makes no sense. Faced with a choice between choosing great people who need to adopt new processes or having great processes but a mediocre team with poorly balanced skills and little aptitude for the job, very few leaders would go for the mediocre team. Clever analysts, incisive researchers, creative Insight managers... these people can bring joy to working in an Insight team and unlock a world of potential for organisations that want to use customer and market understanding to improve business performance.

So, how do Insight leaders improve the situation? The starting point is to map the various aspects involved, and to establish some key principles for each of these areas:

- **The nature of our own roles as Insight leaders:** is leading an Insight team the same as leading any other corporate department, or does it provide some unique challenges that we should recognise and embrace?

- **The skills and attributes of the people in our teams:** which are critical to the roles we need people to play, and which do Insight leaders find it most difficult to find and develop?

- **The Insight perspective that we need to adopt:** beyond skills and attributes, I believe that we should think hard about how our teams look at the world and approach our work with other departments

- **The best ways to recruit Insight people:** given the perspective and the multiple skills and attributes we are looking for, how have successful Insight leaders set about finding new team members?

- **The common issues we have to deal with concerning teamwork:** how do our people work together, and how do we make sure that this generates the best outcomes for our departments?

Having reflected on these issues, we can then think about where we would like to get to, and how far away from that we are at the moment. There is no Insight function in the world that has got every aspect of developing its Insight people completely nailed, but there is a marked difference between the evidence provided by some teams and the norm. Like many other parts of Insight leadership, it is important to keep referring to our Insight strategy so that the way we develop our people plan is consistent with our broader aims.

Finally, I believe it's a question of having the discipline and focus to behave in a way that both supports and inspires our people every day. Too many senior managers talk a great game about leading people when asked specific questions about their approach, or, like the boss I mentioned at the start of this chapter, like to pontificate on the importance of their colleagues when they reflect on their careers. But successful people leadership means routinely prioritising time with our colleagues, embedding our principles through constant repetition, and then considering the unique position of each of our colleagues and the considered advice and authentic support we can offer.

....

The 26th secret of successful Insight teams is that they recognise the importance of developing their Insight people

If you would like to explore this topic further, you might like to read the IMA's Insight leader guide *IMP601: An introduction to developing successful Insight people*

....

Key points to consider:

1. Insight leaders should constantly think about our people, their skills, and how we deploy them
2. Leading Insight people is right up there with leading Insight strategy when it comes to our key responsibilities
3. The starting point is to map critical aspects of people leadership, including the unique nature of our own roles
4. We then need to decide where we are trying to get to in the light of our vision for Insight in our companies
5. We need to devote serious time and attention to working on the people aspect of our roles every day

Many corporate leaders would say that these principles would apply in any management role in any corporate department. I think I would agree, but I also believe that Insight leaders face some specific challenges. So in the next chapter I'm going to challenge you to spend a bit of time thinking about your own role.

Chapter 27
Working on your team not in it

What does an Insight leader actually do? Discussions at the Insight forums suggest that our role is extremely busy and increasingly varied: there are definitely many similarities between Insight leader roles at different organisations, but also key differences. Some of these differences are based on the organisation we work for, or the sector in which our company operates; some are driven by the precise nature of our responsibilities (do you lead a market research-based Insight team, for example, or primarily a group of analysts?). But there are also differences that arise from the choices we make, often subconsciously, and it's those choices about how we define our roles and where we put our time and attention that I'd like to focus on here.

I'm going to suggest that we look at this issue on two axes which we can combine to create a 6-box model. The first axis relates to how much of our time we spend working within our Insight teams – which can quite literally mean sitting at our desks surrounded by close colleagues, or less literally, talking to the people who work for us, or working on the same projects that they are working on. All Insight leaders do this to an extent, but some spend most of their days as 'internal' leaders.

By contrast, other heads of Insight, Research and Analysis choose to spend most of their time as 'external' leaders. Their diaries are full of meetings with other departments and time spent touring the operational sites or stores where customer insights can be used to drive decisions. All Insight leaders do a mixture of both, but the balance varies significantly.

Rather than say that it's the internal or the external side of our roles that is most important at this stage, I'd like to introduce our second axis, because it's looking at these issues through a combination of axes that has proved most valuable to effective leaders.

Running an Insight team is like running a small business

Shortly after joining the IMA I had the opportunity to spend some time in Canada, working on Insight strategy with a great pharmaceutical company in Toronto. I love to read in the evenings when I'm travelling, and I always find that there's something about having physical distance between where you are and the place where you normally work that gives you a different perspective on your job. On this trip I was reading Michael Gerber's *E-myth* books, which are all about running SME businesses, and the more I read, the more I felt that one of Gerber's key frameworks was also useful to Insight leaders. This framework described the different roles that small businesses owners play:

- The technician role
- The managerial role
- The entrepreneurial role

Gerber says that the popular press frequently describes small business owners as entrepreneurs, but in fact most are actually talented technicians who are doing what they do because they have demonstrated their ability to master the technical aspect of previous roles and deliver a product or service to a high standard. If you run a bakery, there's a good chance that you are a talented baker, if you own a small chain of florists, then you are probably great at arranging flowers.

There's nothing wrong with this as such, but the problems arise when the owner of the bakery wants to spend their time still making bread, or the managing director of the florists still wants to act like a florist rather than like an MD. Running a successful SME requires very different skills to working in one, and very different choices about the allocation of time and focus. There is the managerial aspect to consider: the supervision of other people, quality control, keeping the books, ensuring that proper processes are followed. But even more importantly there's the entrepreneurial aspect: envisioning an exciting future for the enterprise, spotting market opportunities, developing new propositions, being alive to market threats and positioning the organisation for success. Critically, Gerber says that successful entrepreneurs 'work on their companies not in them'.

I think there is a strong parallel here with an Insight leader's role, because a large proportion of us have been given our present responsibilities due to the technical ability we have demonstrated as market researchers or analysts. And, unfortunately, I believe that too many of us haven't really moved on and appreciated that being a successful Insight leader requires very different skills and focus to being a successful Insight manager, analyst or researcher.

So let's combine our internal–external axis with Gerber's technical, managerial and entrepreneurial spectrum, and reflect on the choices that Insight leaders make, often subconsciously, about where we spend our time.

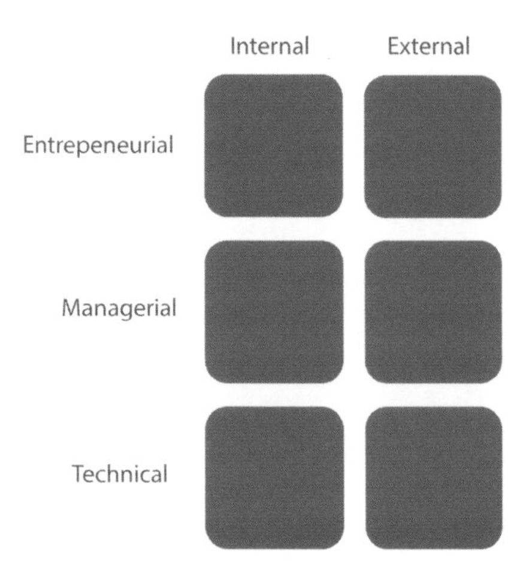

Figure 5: Insight leadership framework

Internal technician role: this might include running research projects or doing analysis, perhaps getting involved in the minutiae of decisions about research sample selection or doing some of the analysis ourselves – the stuff we were always great at if we used to be researchers or analysts.

External technician role: do you find yourself in meetings with other departments presenting work done by others, maybe even explaining what research technique has been used, or the technical reason why the analysis been done one way or another? If so, then you're spending some of your time in this space.

Internal managerial role: this is time spent directly supervising Insight colleagues, checking on their progress, auditing their code, coaching them in technical skills. It might also include time on HR matters: performance management, pay and reward, recruitment and sourcing training.

External managerial role: this relates to conversations about resource allocation with managers from other departments, prioritising which piece of work will be done when, managing expectations, providing project updates to your boss.

Internal entrepreneurial role: this includes reflection on Insight strategy, the motivational side of leadership, time spent painting a picture of success for our Insight colleagues, devising new processes and ways of working to reprioritise our colleagues' time and ensure that maximum effort is put into identifying value and driving change.

External entrepreneurial role: This is about spending time learning from other Insight leaders – or reading this book! It's about selling our vision for Insight to the senior management in our companies, always being on the lookout for new opportunities to promote our department and show how it can add value.

Contrary to what you might expect, I'm not going to tell you that some of these roles are right and some are wrong. I think that all Insight leaders probably need to spend some time playing each role, especially if you have quite a small Insight department. But my challenge to you is to audit your time and be really critical with yourself if you find that your focus is too much on the technical or the managerial. Successful Insight leaders, just like successful business entrepreneurs, need to spend a large portion of their time working on their departments not in them.

....

The 27th secret of successful Insight teams is that they reflect on the many roles of the Insight leader

If you would like to explore this topic further, you might like to read the IMA's Insight leader guide *IMP602: How to lead an Insight team*

....

Key points to consider:

1. Insight leaders should reflect on the internal and external mix of their roles

2. If we have come from a technical background, there is always going to be a temptation to continue to act like technicians

3. Insight leaders, like business owners, also need to be good managers, prioritising work and supervising colleagues

4. Outstanding Insight leaders also embrace the challenge of acting like entrepreneurs: envision future success and go out and grab it

5. Reflect on your time and priorities: we all need to spend more time working on our departments not in them

Having spent time reflecting on our own roles, we can now think about the other jobs to be done in our Insight teams. In the next chapter we'll start with the skills and attributes that distinguish the most effective Insight teams.

Chapter 28
Insight skills and attributes

The calibre of its people is crucial if an Insight team is to perform well. Despite the increasing amount of data available to organisations, and the greater automation of data collection, analysis and reporting, Insight teams continue to need very skilful people who can identify the key insights and business implications, and then influence decision-makers to take the necessary action.

The range of skills needed in an Insight team is growing, mainly because new technology is changing the nature of data collection, data analysis, knowledge management and communication. Progressive organisations are also recognising that by re-purposing their Insight teams as departments that identify value and drive change, they also need to employ people with a more diverse set of skills: Insight consultants, farmers, authors, journalists, storytellers and designers. If our colleagues are going to work on the business and work with the business, they need different attributes to those found in a service function that works *for* the business.

In his book *Good to Great*, Jim Collins makes the point that successful business leaders make it their primary concern to 'get the right people on the bus'. Successful Insight leaders have the same priority.

Categories of skills and attributes

The IMA finds it helpful to think about four main categories of skills and attributes required in an Insight team:

1. Business skills and personal attributes
2. Specific Insight skills
3. Market research skills
4. Insight analysis skills

Since the IMA founded the Insight forum in 2005, there has been much debate about the relative importance of technical skills versus business, personal and investigative skills.

On the one hand, many teams that originally identified themselves as Market Research functions not surprisingly prized the traditional research toolkit as taught in agencies across the world. Some of these teams have started to take a more relaxed view of the need for technical research qualifications now, and instead have prioritised business, personal and generic Insight (or to use David Smith's phrase, 'sense-making') skills. As one Insight leader told us: 'I need consultants who do research, not vice versa.'

On the other hand, the analysis side of the house has been going the other way, with rather mixed results. In the early 2000s, a number of large banks and retailers developed teams founded on business skills and investigative nous, investing in excellent data management systems which reduced the need for expert data analysis. But as the world of data has exploded over the past five years, we have seen a massive increase in the number of data analytics teams with brilliant technical skills, but not necessarily well-rounded business skills.

A related debate over the same time period is the extent to which it is realistic to find 'Insight unicorns', people who can tick all the boxes. A few of the larger Insight teams have taken the approach of dividing team members into two camps: those who focus on technical work and those who focus on the interface with the rest of the business. More commonly, Insight team members are required to have a solid combination of both skillsets, but with space to accommodate people who are stronger in one area than another.

You will have to decide which individual skills and which balance of skillsets is right for your Insight team. But please don't just accept the status quo: look at the skills and attributes needed if your team is going to achieve the potential you have outlined in your Insight strategy, and reflect on the attributes that IMA members themselves have suggested:

Business skills and personal attributes:

- Strategic thinking
- Commercial acumen
- Influencing skills
- Communications skills
- Drive and determination
- Planning
- Problem-solving
- Collaborating
- Positivity

Insight skills and attributes:

- Curiosity

- Passion for customers
- Application of commercial thinking
- Critical thinking and generating hypotheses
- Joining the dots
- Translator
- Storyteller
- Change agent

Specific market research skills:

- Technical skills
- Behavioural psychology and marketing
- Project management skills

Attributes of great Insight analysts:

- Data agnostic
- Focus on the shape of numbers
- Build logical bridges to a solution
- Develop data-driven stories
- Use analysis to paint pictures

....

The 28th secret of successful Insight teams is that they review the skills and attributes that they really need

If you would like to explore this topic further, you might like to read the IMA's Insight leader guide *IMP603: How to identify key Insight skills and attributes*

....

Key points to consider:

1. The calibre of its people is crucial if an Insight team is to perform well

2. Market Research teams were traditionally biased towards technical research skills, but increasingly they now favour broader business skills

3. Data-rich companies created Insight Analysis teams in the early 2000s that prioritised business skills and commercial acumen

4. Companies that have acquired data more recently have too frequently prioritised technical data skills over business skills

5. Reflect on the skills and attributes needed for your team to achieve the potential you have outlined in your Insight strategy

There is another thing that we are looking for in our Insight teams over and above these individual skills and attributes. I'm going to call it an *Insight perspective*, and I'll explain what I mean by that and why it's so important in the next chapter.

Chapter 29

Adopting an Insight perspective

If you work in a corporate Insight role, you might think you know quite a lot about the way the world works. You might be an Insight analyst with long experience looking at patterns in customers' spending; or maybe you're a market researcher, considered by your colleagues to be an expert in understanding the drivers of consumer behaviour.

But how much do we really know about the world around us? About the core stats relating to human life on earth and the trends and changes seen in recent years? Do we have a fact-based worldview, or a set of assumptions backed up by partial insights and incomplete data? For example, how confident are you that you know the answers to these questions:

(a) Where does the majority of the world's population live?

- Low / middle / high income countries?

(b) In the last 20 years, the proportion of the world's population living in extreme poverty has...

- Almost doubled / remained about the same / almost halved

(c) What is the life expectancy of the world's population today?

- 50 years / 60 years / 70 years

(d) There are 2 billion children in the world today aged 0-15 years; how many will there be in the year 2100, according to the UN?

- 2 billion / 3 billion / 4 billion

(e) How did the number of deaths per year from natural disasters change over the last 100 years?

- More than doubled / remained the same / more than halved

These questions, and the answers to them, can be found in a fascinating book called *Factfulness*, written by physician and statistician, Hans Rosling. The quiz has been taken by countless groups of politicians, policy-influencers, corporate executives and students, and the results present a pretty bleak picture. Rosling found that over the course of all the times he had presented the quiz, only 10% of respondents would beat a group of chimpanzees randomly selecting answers. And the more sophisticated an audience, the worse their scores tended to be!

When published in 2018, *Factfulness* instantly gained some high-profile endorsement, especially from Bill Gates who called it 'one of the most important books I've ever read – an indispensable guide to thinking clearly about the world'. Gates rated the book so highly that he reportedly sent every student graduating in the USA in 2018 a free copy.

Hans Rosling, and how he came to write his book

Born in Sweden in 1948, Rosling trained as a doctor and worked in some of the world's most deprived countries. While there, he realised the importance of good information and the difference that an accurate picture of events could play in stopping diseases from spreading. He went on to work with the United Nations, and founded an organisation called the Gapminder Foundation, whose mission is 'to fight devastating ignorance with a fact-based worldview'.

The IMA became aware of Hans Rosling's work some years ago when we referenced him as an expert in data visualisation, and we would recommend all Insight professionals to watch his TED talks and the YouTube clips of his beautifully automated bubble charts. They represent great case studies in how to convey very complex data in an engaging and easy-to-understand format.

But *Factfulness* goes beyond demonstrating how data visualisation can help to communicate insights. Its central message is that:

'People constantly and intuitively refer to their worldview when thinking, guessing or learning. If your worldview is wrong, you will systematically make the wrong guesses.'

It is an uplifting read, demonstrating how the world is usually not as dramatic as you might think, and making the case that there are lots of bad things out there, but far fewer than ever before. Unfortunately, Hans Rosling died before the book could be completed, but the finishing touches were supplied by those who had worked closely with him. This has provided us with what the IMA believes to be one of the most important books ever written about Insight – but which never actually references *Insight* at all.

I will now look at how I think the type of thinking described in *Factfulness* has major implications for corporate Insight teams, and for Insight leaders when they come to recruit and develop their people. But this is no substitute for reading the book itself and I would whole-heartedly recommend that you buy a copy.

Why is *Factfulness* so relevant to the world of corporate Insight?

An important part of my role leading the Insight team at Barclays was to run data-based investigations into critical business issues, supplying decision-makers with facts, figures, insights, ideas and recommendations for how new propositions should be launched, new channels developed, and customer needs addressed.

But it became increasingly apparent over that time that Insight within a global bank, just as in every other sector, is only partly about investigating specific issues. Much of the time it's about challenging assumptions and providing customer and market context. It's about painting a picture to show stakeholders how value is really driven by customer behaviour, and how this behaviour is in turn driven by a wide range of habits, circumstances, beliefs, needs and aspirations. The problem I experienced is not that senior people didn't know particular statistics, it's rather that in a commercial organisation there tends to be an endemic focus on short-term revenue and cost metrics, not on the fundamental truths of how and why customers do business with the organisation.

It's no surprise, then, that in its daily conversations with corporate Insight leaders, the IMA increasingly finds that they have sympathy with Hans Rosling's mission 'to fight devastating ignorance with a fact-based worldview'. Or, in other words, they appreciate the critical need for their teams to develop an *Insight perspective* and share this with senior decision-makers.

If we're going to develop an Insight perspective, and encourage an enhanced corporate worldview shaped by customer and market knowledge, then it is worth going back to Hans Rosling's book. We should consider the application of ten key instincts that he believes are often the barriers to human beings seeing things as they really are.

....

The 29th secret of successful Insight teams is that they adopt an Insight perspective to combat devastating corporate ignorance

If you would like to explore this topic further, you might like to read the IMA's Insight leader guide *IMP604: How to develop an Insight perspective*

....

Key points to consider:

1. How well do you know the core stats relating to human life on earth and the trends and changes seen in recent years?

2. Do you have a fact-based worldview, or a set of assumptions backed up by partial insights and incomplete data?

3. Hans Rosling said that if our worldview is wrong, we will systematically make the wrong guesses

4. This applies in corporate life: many organisations have very incomplete or misleading worldviews about consumers

5. Our researchers and analysts should adopt an Insight perspective and fight devastating ignorance with a fact-based worldview

So far in this section on *Leading Insight* I have looked at the importance of Insight strategy and then the roles and characteristics of our Insight people. The next chapter is the last one in this section, and it's going to focus on some best practice principles for recruiting and developing an Insight team.

Chapter 30
Building an Insight team

In the previous two chapters we have looked at some of the key skills and attributes that effective Insight leaders really value in their teams. In this chapter I will look at best practice in finding, developing and retaining talented people with those characteristics.

Insight team leaders face many daily challenges. People issues are often not seen as being as urgent as the demands of stakeholders until you face a crisis. Yet you need your team to perform at their best in order to deliver what stakeholders need. Furthermore, some corporate policies make recruiting, developing and retaining staff more of a challenge than they used to be: reduced HR support, a blanket ban on the use of specialist recruitment agencies, lower training budgets, flatter team structures, etc. There is a risk that all these things can make recruitment and development seem more like a burden to bear than an opportunity to improve our teams!

Given all of these challenges, how can you find, develop and retain the best talent for your corporate Insight team? As with other topics, we need to give the acquisition and management of people the thought and time it deserves. Specifically:

- Be clear about the skills needed in the team as a whole; audit current skill levels and come up with a long-term plan for closing the gaps

- When you recruit, be clear about the most important skills required and the most effective way to identify the best candidate

- Take a considered approach to on-boarding new staff

- Take the time and trouble to understand what is important to individual team members and how their performance is affected by both their current ability and the opportunities you can give them

- Think creatively to identify workable ways to develop and reward staff

We may not always be in charge of the whole HR process but understanding best practice does give us some ammunition to shape what happens in our organisation. Ultimately, the issue is that if Insight is to deliver competitive advantage, then our organisation must be at least as able as its competitors to recruit, develop and retain really good Insight people.

In the following sections I'm going to set out some of the examples of best practice that IMA members have found most effective.

Insight team recruitment

Insight leaders often find the recruitment process particularly frustrating and far too time-consuming. At worst, they find themselves having to sift through hundreds of applications from unsuitable candidates. They endure a protracted process during which the best people receive other offers, and then find themselves being boxed in by a rigid scoring system. But some of the IMA's corporate members have found approaches you can take which will increase the chances of a smooth, efficient process for everyone involved. These include:

- Be completely clear about which are the absolutely essential skills, experience and qualifications required for the role, and which are only desirable

- Use tactics which will unearth the most suitable applicants; even with corporate policy constraints, there are often still ways to improve the likelihood of success

- Design a process which works for you and the candidates: Insight teams adopt a variety of processes, but most organisations will sift through CVs, conduct an initial screening then arrange assessments in person

- Refine the questions and exercises which really help to pinpoint the best candidate and make sure the process is also clear and transparent to candidates

- Establish the roles that different people will play in the process; it is helpful if several people can be exposed to the candidates at the final assessment stage to give a variety of perspectives

- Agree how the final selection decision will be made: the most methodical approach to identifying the best candidate is for all those involved in the final decision to individually score each candidate on each criterion

Insight team onboarding

The importance of a good experience for a new recruit in their first few weeks in the job is often overlooked. The on-boarding experience can make or break a new hire. Many Insight leaders we speak to in the UK, North America and Europe recognise that it is a challenge to find the time to run inductions properly, but that the investment is worth it in the long run.

- Treat new joiners as you would wish to be treated yourself; never forget that you are welcoming a human being into the fold so make sure that it is clear that you have thought about them and their practical and emotional needs

- Establish what new starters need to know in month one; many Insight teams have a checklist or pack of information that new starters need to be exposed to early on

- Agree how new starters can best understand what the organisation does; for example, British Gas new joiners experience a day with a service engineer and a day in a call centre whilst new recruits at Lucozade Ribena Suntory visit a factory to experience drinks production

- Decide the best way for new starters to meet key stakeholders; most Insight leaders see meeting key stakeholders as a critical part of the early induction process

- Decide how soon to set formal targets: in a number of organisations, a 3-month probationary period is a standard part of the employment process for any role, but this requires clear target setting to measure performance at the end of that period

Insight team development

It is important that your team members have the opportunity to develop their skills, knowledge and experience. Development helps staff to perform better, and it helps to maintain their job satisfaction.

- Make development a priority and diarise a regular time for it

- Put in the time to really get to know each of your team members, their backgrounds, their family situations, and what makes them tick

- Ensure individuals are stimulated and stretched because most Insight team members want to do work that they find interesting and to learn new things or new skills

- Find creative ways to reward people because flat structures and small teams present challenges for pay rises and other monetary rewards

Team recruitment and development is a complex area and you will probably have your own preferred tactics and approaches. But if you would like to explore the ideas set out here in more detail then it's worth speaking to other Insight leaders or consulting the IMA's online guides.

....

The 30th secret of successful Insight teams is that they take a progressive approach to recruitment, onboarding and team development

If you would like to explore this topic further, you might like to read the IMA's Insight leader guide *IMP605: How to recruit and develop an Insight team*

....

Key points to consider:

1. Large corporate organisations sometimes make Insight team recruitment and development more difficult than we would like
2. We must not see it as a burden but as a great opportunity to improve our Insight capability
3. Recruitment in particular provides us with a chance to bring in new talent and alter the shape of our resources
4. Most departments do not give sufficient thought to on-boarding, but this can be crucial for establishing good working relationships
5. When it comes to developing our colleagues we must consider their specific circumstances, needs and aspirations

This chapter concludes our focus on *Leading Insight*. But if we really want to transform our Insight teams and their role, there are a few more ways we can optimise impact on our organisations' performance. These relate to the position of Insight in our companies, and the extent to which we are aligned with the organisation's key outcomes. We'll consider both in the fourth section, *Optimising Impact*.

Section 4

Optimising the impact of Insight

Optimising the impact of Insight

In the fourth section of *Transforming Insight,* we will focus on the next ten secrets of successful corporate Insight teams:

Chapter 31
Optimising impact through positioning

A few years ago I was chairing the client-side stream of the Market Research Summit in London and I had a chat over coffee with the Head of Insight at one of the UK's largest estate agents. We were discussing some of the presentations we had heard from leading brands that morning and the great work that corporate Insight teams were doing. We agreed that in more and more companies the Insight team now had the potential to really drive change and transform their organisation's performance, but all too often structural issues seemed to get in the way. Many Insight leaders felt that their team were doing the right things, but that getting Insight noticed and acted upon was like pushing water uphill.

But having agreed on the general difficulties, this Insight leader then surprised me: she said that although she thought that optimising impact was really difficult for most Insight teams, in her company it was actually very easy. I was intrigued! What great influencing technique had she discovered? How had she framed her Insight strategy? Were her analysts and researchers just better than those in other Insight departments?

No, the answer was rather more mundane: she said that they had a small head office with an open plan layout, and her desk was directly opposite the CEO. Every morning he would ask her what the Insight team had discovered the day before, and why she thought it was important, and for the rest of the day the CEO would quiz his fellow directors on their understanding of these latest insights and ask what they were going to do about them...

Initially, I'm afraid I was rather disappointed. I don't know how many Insight leaders reading this book sit next to their CEO – I'm not sure how many would want to – but on the face of it, this didn't feel like a strategy that many of us could use to transform the effectiveness of our Insight teams.

But during the rest of the conference I kept thinking about the conversation, and the more I thought about it, the more profound it seemed. This Insight team was getting traction because they found themselves in a great position in the organisation – literally, sitting next to the CEO. Other Insight leaders would probably not have that particular opportunity, but that didn't mean that we shouldn't obsessively seek to improve the positioning of Insight, as a concept and as a department, in the hearts, minds and processes of all our companies.

Insight as a lighthouse

An Insight team should look outwards to an organisation's customers and markets and shine a light on issues of strategic importance. In stormy weather, it is there to pinpoint rocks upon which the organisation might founder, and competitor companies with which the company might collide. Many Insight teams pride themselves on their ability to understand customer behaviour and its drivers. They have developed a powerful light to shine upon market issues, and they aspire to serve as a lighthouse, a beacon to guide their organisation as it navigates the market.

However, a lighthouse helps nobody if it is not in a position to be seen. Positioned inland, or hidden by cliffs, its light cannot help shipping. Likewise, there is little point in building an Insight capability to identify issues and guide management teams along the best route if our Insight teams are not well *positioned* within our companies.

Effective Insight teams succeed in identifying and occupying an optimal position in the hearts, minds and processes of their wider organisation. If an

Insight team is widely perceived to be critical to taking key business decisions, then decision-makers will automatically consult the Insight team to help nail business questions and to find an answer to them.

If your Insight team has a strong position, it also makes the team's job a lot easier. You can prioritise work without being overruled; you can turn your Insight strategy into a practical reality with less challenge; you can invest time and money farming customer knowledge as well as generating new insights. Decision-makers seek your input rather than batting away meeting requests.

Some Insight teams are lucky and already find themselves in a corporate culture or structure that automatically gives Insight a strong position. For instance, you might work in a relatively small, centralised organisation and have a team leader in a senior position with direct access to the C-suite.

Most Insight teams, though, have to work hard to achieve a strong position. As a result, when benchmarked, Insight leaders tend to give their team a relatively low score on Insight positioning compared to other aspects.

Insight positioning can be an existential issue. An Insight team with a strong position is much less vulnerable to reorganisations and cutbacks. It can make evidence-based decisions about the role it will play in the future; it will be far more likely to drive genuine change on a regular basis; and it will also be able to provide worthwhile and satisfying careers for its team members.

So how can we position Insight for success?

The last 15 years have shown that there are four possible pathways to putting Insight in a better position, plus a fifth that we should all think about going forwards. They are not mutually exclusive, but we do need to decide which pathway to prioritise.

I will explore the first four of these pathways in the next four chapters of this book, and we'll come back to the final pathway in chapter 41.

....

The 31st secret of successful Insight teams is that they optimise their impact by improving their position in hearts, minds and processes

If you would like to explore this topic further, you might like to read the IMA's Insight leader guide *IMP701: An introduction to successful Insight positioning*

....

Key points to consider:

1. Insight teams, like lighthouses, help nobody if they are not in a position to be seen
2. Many Insight leaders believe that their teams get less traction than they should, despite all their hard work
3. There are often structural barriers to Insight becoming more effective, and some may appear impossible to shift
4. We should become obsessive about improving the position of Insight in the hearts, minds and processes of our wider organisation
5. Successful Insight leaders have discovered five possible pathways to improve the position of their Insight team

In chapter 17 I suggested that Insight leaders needed to act like the Chief Marketing Officers for their departments, and design a programme of communication considering key audiences, content and channels. In the next chapter we'll return to the theme of marketing Insight, but this time we're going to focus on the Insight brand in your company.

Chapter 32
Developing the Insight brand

There is no point producing any research or analysis unless it drives change. So, forward-looking Insight teams think carefully about how they are going to disseminate their insights and ideas. As we saw in section 2, *Driving Change,* the IMA's most effective corporate members have developed:

- **Influencing skills** and plans to help them to persuade specific decision-makers to follow their recommendations, and

- **Communication skills** and plans to enable them to share customer and market knowledge throughout the organisation

To borrow a marketing analogy, this is rather like a company focusing on selling to key clients, and also developing advertising to communicate the benefits of its products across a broad market. Both are established tactics, but they are both much easier if the company has first developed a well-respected brand. According to the entrepreneur.com website:

'An effective brand strategy gives you a major edge in increasingly competitive markets. But what exactly does "branding" mean? Simply put, your brand is your promise to your customer. It tells them what they can expect from your products and services, and it differentiates your offering from that of your competitors. Your brand is derived from who you are, who you want to be and who people perceive you to be.'

In our world of corporate Insight, we might rephrase that paragraph as:

'What differentiates Insight and the Insight team from other functions in our organisation? An effective brand strategy gives us a major advantage in making our voice heard. Simply put, our Insight brand is our promise to our internal customers. It tells them what they can expect from our products and services, and it differentiates our offering from that of other functions. Our brand is derived from who we are, who we want to be and who people perceive us to be.'

All Insight teams already have a brand of some sort whether we realise it or not. Unless they have never heard of us at all, other departments will have a view of what we do, how that activity affects them, and whether they think that is useful or not. There's a very good chance that if you've never tried to actively manage people's perceptions of your department, there are probably going to be quite a few different views of Insight as both a concept and a team. And it's quite possible that none of them really align with the Insight team's view of itself or, perhaps more importantly, the view that you would really like other departments to have going forward.

There is an important link here to Insight strategy, and your vision for what role Insight could play in your organisation. In section 3, *Leading Insight*, I said that this vision should be developed from an analysis of the opportunities for Insight to make a difference, and your level of ambition to seize those opportunities. Developing your Insight brand involves taking your vision and mission statement and then working out how to create an effective perception of Insight and its role in the hearts and minds of your potential customers. If an Insight strategy is our teams' equivalent of a company's corporate strategy, then our brand development is the equivalent of a company thinking about its marketing positioning.

Prioritising brand development

Many Insight professionals are very familiar with the concept of brand in relation to their organisation. We know that it's a shortcut to understanding the promise of what is on offer. It takes time to develop, and requires a lot of conscious, focused effort and investment to build.

Some Insight professionals will have been actively involved in developing and measuring their company's brand. Many market researchers will have helped test brand values, authenticity, and positioning. You may also have been involved in brand tracking, to ensure everyone in the organisation lives up to those values.

However, though most Insight teams are involved in some sort of brand activity on behalf of their organisation, most of us have given little thought to our own Insight team's brand. Take a brief moment to think about what the brand promise of your Insight team within your organisation says about you. Understanding how stakeholders perceive the Insight team is really important, because it is that perception that helps to shape the team's positioning in the eyes of other functions.

Should brands differentiate product offerings or just make them distinctive? Byron Sharp, in his book *How Brands Grow*, says that success comes from being distinctive than rather than differentiated. So, what distinctive assets does your team have compared to other functions? Is it the way you ask good questions and listen? Is it your use of multiple data sources? Is it your unique access to a customer database or consumer panel? Is it your operational and commercial understanding? What you decide the distinctive brand characteristics are will be a matter of judgement, but it's important to reflect carefully on which of those characteristics are most important and which make your team distinct. Remember, an Insight team brand is only a means to an end, so this is not about promoting your department for the sake of it; it's about managing perceptions of what the department stands for, and the role it plays in your company.

One final thing to consider is how your personal brand is aligned to your vision for the team. Strong Insight leaders can become well-known within their organisations and this can be an enormous benefit – some of the most progressive leaders at the IMA's Insight forums really embody all that is good about their departments. But it can also be a disadvantage if the top Insight professional has so much personal recognition that their department's brand exists only in the leader's shadow; several IMA members have scored themselves highly on brand development only for the senior leader to leave and them to recognise too late that there was a strong 'brand Suzy' but very little 'brand Insight'.*

So, whether you have consciously worked on it or not, the team will have a brand; colleagues in other departments will have some sort of perception of what you do. Now is the time to actively develop and manage the perception of Insight and its role in the hearts and minds of your potential customers.

*Please don't be offended if you are called Suzy

....

The 32nd secret of successful Insight teams is that they actively develop the brand of Insight and the Insight team within their company

If you would like to explore this topic further, you might like to read the IMA's Insight leader guide *IMP702: How to develop the Insight brand*

....

Key points to consider:

1. If you want to improve the position of your Insight team, one of the most effective pathways is to focus on your Insight team brand

2. All Insight teams have a brand, so reflect on what it says about you at the moment and whether this is what you would like it to be

3. Many Insight professionals will have worked on your corporate brand; you can tap into this expertise to enhance your team brand

4. An Insight team brand is only a means to an end, so this is not about promoting your department for the sake of it

5. As individuals, we should also be aware of our personal brands, and use our own profile to role-model the right behaviours

All Insight leaders should think about the Insight brand in their organisation, but, just as with our organisations themselves, there is no point in spending hours on the nuances of brand if nobody has actually heard of our team in the first place. Sometimes it's better to focus on awareness, and that's what we'll do in the next chapter.

Chapter 33
Promoting awareness

In the previous chapter, I suggested that Insight leaders should think about their departments like companies in a market and recognise the important role that brand can play in framing perceptions. This goes beyond visual cues like logos or straplines; it includes reflection on team purpose, the promise we are making to other departments, and the positive and negative impacts that our personal brands can have on other people's perceptions.

However, many Insight leaders have probably watched from the touchline as marketing teams have debated the finer nuances of what their brands should stand for, getting terribly excited about details which probably mean far more to some of the people within their companies than to most of the consumers in their market. And there's no point developing detailed brand concepts if nobody has heard of our companies in the first place.

So it is with the internal positioning of our Insight teams. We should certainly reflect on our Insight brand, but also recognise that we often simply need to promote awareness of Insight as a concept and our team as a department. This requires an opportunistic mindset as our internal market for Insight is always changing. It is very easy to assume that everyone knows who we are, but in a large company they probably don't, and we have to start again every time there is a major reorganisation or new senior managers arrive.

In its work on influencing decision-makers, the IMA has looked at the busy world in which senior managers live and work (see chapter 12). We recognise that corporate executives are under a lot of pressure and big decisions involve both business and personal risk. Senior people operate in a very crowded information landscape.

In a consumer world, when we are under pressure and there is too much information out there to get our heads around, we turn to familiar organisations. We haven't got time to search for others or evaluate what they have to offer, so we stick to the tried and tested. The same is true for internal stakeholders. The more pressure they are under, the less time they have, and the more competing voices they hear, the more they will rely on the people and departments that are top-of-mind for advice. Sometimes, that simply means they will turn to the advisers that everyone else turns to. If we want that to be us, how can we promote awareness of Insight and our Insight teams?

What is best practice?

The IMA's work with Insight teams across the world provides a good starting point for any Insight leader who wants to promote their team. Our members' experience suggests that we should:

- Adopt an ambitious mindset: go to work every day intent on making our team and its work more famous in our companies
- Remain alert for every opportunity to promote our team
- Put ourselves in a good position to spot opportunities
- Re-engineer our team activity plans so that we can take advantage of sudden opportunities
- Target senior directors and plan for how we can raise awareness at the top

- Work closely with our internal communication team as this can add credibility and professionalism

- Be prepared to be proactive and creative

Individual members have found more specific ways that have helped them. For example, the Insight team at UK retailer Marks & Spencer held a 2-week Customer Insight Festival which 1,700 colleagues attended. Another Insight team, at international financial services firm Legal & General, embarked on an Insight Roadshow, showcasing their work on older consumers at all their company's head office sites. This included fun elements like using an app to show what their young colleagues would look like when they reached retirement – nothing to do with Insight you might say, but a brilliant way of engaging head office teams and helping them to appreciate that older people's needs were very different from their own.

The larger the organisation, the more difficult it is to become well-known, especially if you have a small team. Realistically you cannot do bespoke work to support very many business projects. One of the ways that members have sought to overcome a disadvantage like this is to identify and then promote *signature* pieces of work – projects that demonstrate our ability to produce insights that are both memorable and useful to decision-makers. Classic examples are customer segmentations, analysis of future trends, and brand repositioning research. Awareness can be highly affected by just one or two pieces of exceptionally impactful work, so if you have a piece of work like that on your hands, make sure you shout about it! The work does not always have to represent typical team output; the type of analysis or research is probably less important than the profile of the business initiative.

One example of this working well has been at Transport for London where the Insight team have promoted their work on Customer Pain Points. This got a lot of traction with senior stakeholders because it resonated with them; everyone who works in the transport industry has the daily experience of friends and family telling them about travel disaster stories, so it tapped into a familiar theme. Another example comes from one of my IMA colleagues,

Tim Downing, when he was Insight and Foresight Director at international brewers Molson Coors. They identified the potential of a project on consumer trends and set out to roadshow the findings as widely as possible. Again, this piece resonated with decision-makers because it related to trends that they could recognise as consumers themselves. It wasn't difficult to get engagement.

When I worked at Barclays one of my favourite signature pieces was the annual report that we sent to every branch manager, full of colourful maps and charts explaining their local market and the opportunity that existed to grow their share of business. This Insight project tapped into a prevailing passion at Barclays - that head office was there to support the branch network - and because there was a physical output, a glossy report, the project leant itself to all sorts of promotional activities. These included sending the CEO a copy of the specific report for each branch just before she visited it, or the Insight team carrying copies of the reports into other meetings and dropping them on the table as conversation-starters.

....

The 33rd secret of successful Insight teams is that they constantly look for ways of promoting awareness of Insight

If you would like to explore this topic further, you might like to read the IMA's Insight leader guide *IMP703: How to promote awareness of Insight*

....

Key points to consider:

1. Clever ideas about your Insight team's brand will be a waste of time if few people in your company know that the Insight team exists
2. Building awareness requires an entrepreneurial and opportunistic mindset: we must identify every promotion opportunity
3. Promoting Insight is not always easy so it requires a proper plan for reaching key stakeholders with chosen messages
4. Identify and promote key signature pieces of work with which your department can become synonymous
5. Great signature pieces relate to an issue of the moment, contain a fundamental truth, and link directly to commercial outcomes

The more that senior people are aware of the Insight team and its capabilities, the more likely you are to be invited to advise on more strategic pieces of work. But there's no point in winning those opportunities if the work you produce then lets you down. Sometimes we can best improve the position of our team by focusing on its reputation for great delivery, so that's what we'll look at in the next chapter.

Chapter 34
Improving your reputation

It is important to think about your brand – what you want Insight and the Insight team to stand for – and to promote greater awareness of your team and its capabilities. But there is no point in doing either, if people's practical experience of working with the Insight team has been poor or undermines the impression you would have wanted to create.

In marketing terms, it's like a company spending millions advertising its brand and promoting awareness of its services, only to find that the user experience lets them down. If you have had a bad experience with a company, it really doesn't matter what you think of their advertising. Marketing claims can also be undermined by other people talking about their poor experience, or indeed by negative press coverage. I have a vivid memory of speaking at some marketing and research conferences in Paris and Brussels in the early 2000s when Barclays multi-million dollar advertising campaign 'a big bank for a big world' had just been fatally undermined by a press announcement that we were closing 150 branches in the UK! A company is known by its actions as well as its words, and it has to make sure the two are aligned.

The same thinking has to apply to our Insight teams. Yes, we should define our brand and promote our team, but we must also be careful that we earn a reputation in our internal market that is consistent with the image that we want to promote. There are two aspects of this to consider: doing things right, and doing the right things.

Doing things right

Insight professionals tend to be very conscientious, with most analysts and market researchers priding themselves on doing a good job and on being seen to do a good job. That doesn't always mean that it's easy to establish a reputation for doing things right, because every company I know expects its Insight team to produce more work than they can realistically deliver to a good standard. If you remember the Insight leadership matrix from chapter 27, the senior Insight professional in most organisations has to spend more time than they would like on 'external management' tasks – meeting with stakeholders, prioritising resources, managing expectations about how soon work can be completed, etc.

Therefore, there is always room to improve other departments' perceptions of the Insight function as an agile, knowledgeable, technically competent group of specialists who always deliver what they say they will on time and on budget. And just like in the consumer world of service delivery, it's the emotional things that count as much as the rational things: do stakeholders enjoy working with your team, or do they come to you for support because they have to? Are they drawn to working with you because they respect your customer knowledge, or because they like being in meetings with you? Do they trust your department to solve problems for them without giving them a hard time for not remembering what you told them last month? As we saw in section 2, *Driving Change*, senior decision-makers will inevitably engage most with those they find credible and reliable, but also those with whom they have an appropriate level of intimacy.

Doing the right things

However, there is a bigger challenge to consider: the Insight service trap. Driven by a natural desire to please, too many Insight teams bend over backwards to accommodate requests for data, facts and figures. Some of this is necessary to win friends and influence people, but the problem comes when our efforts to provide a great service consolidate other departments' historic perception that Insight is a service function. It's no good defining our teams as the group that will use customer and market knowledge to identify value for our companies and drive change within them if the practical experience of working with us is that we just say yes when asked for information.

This is a real issue for both small, young teams and larger, more mature teams. In a new function it is common to find relatively junior researchers and analysts who have technical skills but less business experience. In a more mature team, the habit of working as a service function can be hard to shift, and at times of stress and hyperactivity (in other words most of the time in some companies!) we all tend to revert to type. So as progressive Insight leaders we have to put a lot of time and effort into establishing our department's reputation not only for doing things right, but for doing the right things. We will not be able to optimise impact by improving the position of Insight in our organisations if the practical experience of working with our weakest analyst or most junior researcher is not aligned to our team purpose.

What is best practice?

Some of the most effective Insight teams have confronted this challenge with a mix of team processes, standards and structure:

- UK lottery provider Camelot is one of many to have focused on Insight team workflow, encouraging junior and middle management to self-serve via the Insight intranet for facts and figures, thus leaving their Insight managers to focus on genuine business investigations.

- The famous bakers, Warburtons, are amongst several Insight teams to set up a team email account so that they can respond to new requests in a consistent way. Even larger global organisations like Visa have achieved the same end by using their Insight portals as the gateway for logging new requests and cutting out the inconsistency inherent in requests coming in to multiple team members.

- International energy company SSE re-structured their team away from primary and secondary research so that individuals could focus on specific business areas and become familiar with the big commercial challenges.

- The giant supermarket group, Tesco, have looked for innovative ways to celebrate success and focus attention on the right behaviours. This has included 'BOEING of the month' awards for those who have sized business issues in a creative way (see chapter 4).

....

The 34th secret of successful Insight teams is that they manage their reputation for doing things right and doing the right things

If you would like to explore this topic further, you might like to read the IMA's Insight leader guide *IMP704: How to improve your Insight team's reputation*

....

Key points to consider:

1. Developing an Insight brand and raising awareness of Insight can be undermined by the experience of working with your team
2. All Insight professionals want to do a good job and be seen to be doing a good job, but there is always scope to do things better
3. Senior decision-makers will choose to work with the departments that they like as well as those they respect
4. Beware the service trap: you need to manage your team's reputation for doing the right things as well as doing things right
5. Consider the right standards for your team, optimise workflows, reward the right behaviours, and structure around business issues

Focusing on this third pathway to optimise impact by improving the position of your team is complimentary to the first two pathways, Brand and Awareness. But the fourth pathway represents another option, one that doesn't start with the Insight team but rather with the wider organisation. This is what we'll look at in the next chapter.

Chapter 35
Respecting the rhythms and rituals

So far in this section we have considered three possible pathways to optimise Insight's impact through its positioning. We have looked at developing a brand that is consistent with our aspirations; also at promoting awareness of Insight; and how both brand and awareness can be undermined if the reputation created by the experience of working with us is poor.

However, Byron Sharp's incisive work on marketing effectiveness has reminded us that it is physical availability that drives many consumer decisions – put simply, you buy it if you need it and it's there. This is true for Insight in our organisations as well. Senior executives are going to make decisions regardless of whether they can get all the support and advice they would like at that moment in time. They have their own timescales, and our companies have their own rhythms and rituals of how they do things. The harsh reality is that they will often include Insight if it is in front of them and looks like it will add value at the right moment. But if it isn't, they will proceed regardless, and maybe only come to the Insight team late in the day asking for confirmatory facts and figures. By that time it's often too late for us to influence the main debate without looking as if we're being negative.

So, the fourth pathway to improving the position of our Insight teams is to stop focusing on ourselves and look outwards. Let's familiarise ourselves with our company's rhythms and rituals, and then figure out how, when and where Insight can intervene to guide decisions.

Which processes should we consider?

The first step is to identify the most important business decisions being taken within an organisation and look at the processes involved. There will be a business planning cycle, a sales reporting cycle, a budgeting cycle, a whole programme of activity driven by when key committees meet. In parallel there will be dates when new management information becomes available, or when it needs to be submitted.

What are the rhythms and rituals in your company? What are the formal processes? Are these set in stone, or do they change each time the business re-structures? Does your organisation have a well-developed set of formal processes or is it far more informal – even chaotic – about the way it makes decisions? We should consider the informal processes and networks that it might be even more important to recognise. As we saw in chapter 12, the better we understand the world of senior decision-makers, the more likely we are to appreciate what they need from us. The IMA's Emma Jones, formerly at retailer Halfords, says we should consider:

a) What the big decisions are likely to be

b) Who makes these decisions

c) How often these decisions are made

d) Where the big decisions are made

Every organisation will be unique in precisely how it makes decisions, but companies will have similarities, especially those operating within the same sector.

- **Business planning:** retailers often have an annual planning process, with a financial plan preceding a trading plan, and – in the best – a customer plan preceding the financial plan. Waitrose supermarket, part of John Lewis & Partners, is one example of an Insight team devoting a significant amount of effort into developing the customer plan each year, seeing it as an annual opportunity to shape the rest of the company's thinking.

- **New product development process (NPD):** especially relevant in the FMCG world, many Insight teams try to secure a recognised place in the NPD cycle, with analysis and research feeding into decisions at key stages. One company, chocolate manufacturer Thorntons, now part of the Ferrero group, found that they were often consulted too late in the NPD process so they argued for the inclusion of a new stage in the process, Gate 0, when the Insight team were mandated to provide high-level confirmation that a product idea would find a large enough market before funding for the product was agreed.

- **Marketing planning:** another classic role for Insight teams is in the marketing planning process, with analysts identifying customer segments, and researchers investigating customer needs. Market research often plays into both strategic brand planning and more tactical advertising development. Some Insight teams go further than this and play a critical role identifying direct mail and email targets. There is nothing wrong with this in principle, but if your Insight team becomes synonymous with CRM and direct marketing activity it is unlikely that you are devoting enough attention to strategic decisions. Too much responsibility for tactical and operational activity leads to recruiting data analysts rather than Insight analysts, and the term *Insight* itself becomes shorthand for data-based operations instead of driving key strategic decisions.

So which pathway is most important? The answer inevitably is that it depends on the current position of your Insight team, and on the position you aspire to occupy. But ten years ago I was put on the spot whilst speaking at a conference in Sydney and found myself saying that if I could only pick one pathway, for me it would be the last one: understanding my organisation's decision-making processes. Many years later we held a vote at two of the IMA's Insight forums: in London, members also voted for the Process pathway, in Manchester they came down in favour of Reputation.

....

The 35th secret of successful Insight teams is that they improve their role in key organisational processes

If you would like to explore this topic further, you might like to read the IMA's Insight leader guide *IMP705: How to improve Insight's role in key processes*

....

Key points to consider:

1. The first three pathways focus on our Insight teams' brand, awareness and reputation, the fourth on the wider organisation
2. There is a neat symmetry here: Insight encourages organisations to focus first on their market, so why shouldn't we?
3. All companies will have their unique rhythms and rituals, but there will often be similarities, especially within sectors
4. The aim is for Insight to be consulted as the default option: it is so much easier than arguing for your inclusion project by project
5. If there are few established processes in your company it is best practice to create some, with Insight involved at critical stages

We'll return to the topic of Insight positioning in chapter 41, but before we get there we need to look at another aspect of *Optimising Impact*. This is commerciality or, if you think that you work for an organisation that isn't commercial, alignment with finance and business objectives.

Chapter 36
Optimising impact through commerciality

What does it mean to be commercial? Is it about having passed your accountancy exams? Or perhaps having the ability to sell used cars? Or being experienced in leading Sales teams? Perhaps it's about having the unshakeable inner confidence that if you were in the boardroom on The Apprentice TV show, you would be hired, not fired?

At the IMA's 55th Insight forum in London, we discussed this topic with Insight leaders from 40 leading organisations, including eBay, Nestle, Premier Foods and Tesco. Many of the Insight leaders present had felt pressure from their organisations to 'become more commercial' and some felt that they were making progress. But the overall sense was that this is an area that Insight teams do not find easy, a subject at which we feel we ought to be better than we are. Or maybe one that we'd rather ignore... please could we just focus on understanding customers better and leave the commercial stuff to the Sales people?

One thing is for sure: of all the territories that the IMA encourages Insight leaders to explore, this is the one where collectively we feel there is the most work still to do. That's not just a gut feeling: when benchmarked, Insight teams score an average of only 4.9 points out of 12 on Insight commerciality, making this the weakest territory out of the eight assessed in the IMA's Insight benchmark.

I think it's time to reframe the question and change the way that Insight teams think about commerciality. Let's forget the image of the used car salesman and think about a simple interaction between two people standing at a market stall selling vegetables. Every commercial interaction involves three elements:

- A customer
- A supplier
- An exchange of value

Because many of us work in head office environments we usually don't see customer interactions with our own eyes, and we can lose sight of the essential simplicity of them. We can therefore be blind to a key insight - our organisations cannot have real commercial understanding unless they have great insights about all three elements in our market stall example:

- They need to know the customer, who she is, what she needs, why she chose this stall today and how she will pick what to buy
- They need to understand themselves - the market trader in our example - how he manages his overheads and sources his products, the cost of producing those vegetables and selling them
- They need to understand the transactions that take place, the volume of goods sold, the price paid, and the margin made

This understanding can only come from joining the dots across customer data, operational data and financial data.

How does this affect the Insight team?

Working in an Insight team it can often be tempting to think that the commercial aspects of a business are somebody else's concern. We construct a view of the world which separates the *commercial* from the *customer*.
This means that the idea of researchers and analysts being commercial feels akin to putting on somebody else's uniform or accepting a different mindset.

Not only do we think of rational reasons for rejecting the idea, some of us might feel an emotional reaction, maybe even recoil from the suggestion that we'd have to accept another department's motives and values.

But an organisation cannot be considered commercial, let alone achieve sustainable commercial success, without understanding the customer, its own operations, and the financial transactions between customer and supplier. And so the learning developed by an Insight team is just as integral to the whole concept of commerciality as the spreadsheets kept by Finance or the operational processes developed by Product, Sourcing, Marketing and Sales teams.

Commercial success = customer + operations + finance

Insight is crucial to commercial success because it supplies the customer aspect of this equation. However, you could argue that our role is actually even more important, because Insight people are naturally skilled at joining together data and ideas from multiple sources and putting them together to form a model of behaviour. It is often easier for us to consider the financial and operational data we would need for our commercial models, than it is for other departments to understand which key customer and market insights they need to integrate into theirs.

Therefore, if you are a corporate Insight leader who wants to optimise the impact of your team, the questions to ask are not:

- Should my Insight team become more commercial?
- How do I persuade my colleagues to accept that this must happen?

But rather they are:

- How can Insight improve my organisation's commercial understanding?

- What tools and behaviours can my Insight team develop to help my company?

Does this whole concept only apply in an organisation whose ultimate purpose is to make a profit for shareholders? If you work in a public sector or not-for-profit organisation, can you avoid thinking about any financial and operational data?

The answer to both questions is 'no'. All organisations require some degree of financial accounting to measure income versus expenditure, and understanding this picture, and the organisation's internal workings, is just as important for an Insight team in a charity or a government department as in a commercial company. Insight work has to be harnessed to the aim of long-term, sustainable success, and this cannot be done effectively if the Insight team focus solely on customer issues and ignore the connection to its operations and finances.

....

The 36th secret of successful Insight teams is that they recognise that they are integral to their organisation's sustainable financial success

If you would like to explore this topic further, you might like to read the IMA's Insight leader guide *IMP801: An introduction to Insight commerciality*

....

Key points to consider:

1. We must put aside the idea that Insight teams can focus on the customer and leave others to worry about the commercial
2. Every successful company understands its customers, its internal operations, and the finances of supplying customers with a service
3. Progressive Insight teams are well-placed to join the dots between customer, financial and operational data
4. The language is different in the not-for-profit and public sector but understanding income and expenditure is still vital
5. The key question is: 'How can Insight teams help their organisations achieve sustainable financial success?'

The next four chapters of this section on *Optimising Impact* will develop the idea of Insight commerciality. The first step is to build a commercial foundation, so that's what we'll explore in the next chapter.

Chapter 37
Building commercial foundations

A company cannot expect sustainable commercial success unless it develops and leverages an expert understanding of its own operational performance, its customers' behaviour, and the financial outcome of customers' interaction with the organisation. This is very unlikely to happen in a large company if the Insight function doesn't recognise that its work is integral to commercial success. For this recognition to make a tangible difference, however, the Insight leaders need to build a commercial foundation for the work carried out by our departments.

What does a commercial foundation look like?

From its work with Insight teams from across all industry sectors in the UK, Europe and North America, the IMA believes that a commercial foundation requires us to put together a body of knowledge and understanding comprising four elements:

1. The assembly of **Core Stats**

    - Internal facts and figures concerning how the organisation makes money

    - External facts and figures relating to why the organisation makes money in that market

To collate the internal Core Stats, most Insight teams will have to reach out to other departments like Finance and Operations. Insight teams that have a comprehensive customer database will have a natural advantage if they can link customers to transactions, to the cost of producing those services, and to the revenue derived from them. Insight teams that operate in sectors like FMCG will only be able to do this at an aggregate, segment level. However, all Insight teams should be able to collate good external Core Stats like market size, market share, average basket size in each market, or average number of product holdings because there's a good chance that we will be responsible for sourcing these for our company anyway.

2. The development of a **Business Blueprint**, which:

    - Outlines the parts and processes of the organisation that result in the delivery of a product or service to a customer

    - Maps the external market to show the circumstances that drive customers to do business in that way with that organisation

    - Identifies the linkages between different 'nodes' in this model to illustrate how a change in one measure might have a knock-on effect on another (e.g. a rise in brand awareness leading to more purchase consideration, or a decrease in bank branches leading to a decline in new accounts being opened)

The IMA recommends that Insight teams frame their Business Blueprints using the *MADE in Insight* model that we explored in chapter 3, mapping from the market to the money. If our Insight managers, analysts and researchers can habitually consider the wider implications of the specific customer behaviours and attitudes that they study, then compiling a Business Blueprint becomes a routine activity rather than a one-off piece of work.

3. Insights about **dynamics, trends, opportunities and threats**

   The Insight team will then want to overlay quantitative and qualitative insights about the key dynamics and trends that it uncovers in its research and analysis. What is changing? What do we think might happen next year? This is clearly not a one-off exercise, as each substantive piece of work should add to the team's knowledge of customer behaviour and its drivers. However, building a commercial foundation will definitely require extra effort at the outset.

4. An **Executive Brief** which describes the Core Stats, their role in the Business Blueprint, and the key trends and dynamics.

   Writing a briefing document or summary presentation is a great way to crystallise the understanding inherent in our commercial foundation. It also makes it a tangible deliverable that we can present to existing management or an incoming senior director. Not only will this help executives to understand how consumers in our market become customers of our organisation and produce a commercial return, it will also help to prioritise the foundation building ahead of other Insight projects. This helps to combat the inevitable temptation to postpone foundational work until we are less busy (a fantasy time that will obviously never arrive!).

Developing a commercial mindset

To really accelerate Insight commerciality it is also important to encourage our Insight managers, researchers and analysts to adopt a more commercial mindset. IMA members have identified various ideas to facilitate this, including:

- Look out for news stories that have an impact on your market and set aside time as a team to discuss them. Even better, encourage your colleagues to talk about these issues informally around their desks, recognising that how your organisation interacts with consumers in your market should be a key focus for everyone in Insight.

- Encourage curiosity about how your organisation's operations are organised. We all roll our eyes when the latest restructure is announced, but the way that companies set about the task of creating and delivering services to customers is another key part of the commercial jigsaw. When making commercial recommendations, Insight needs to take account of costs, and also reflect the feasibility of doing things differently.

- A commercial mindset demands realism about the key decision-making dynamics within your company. Is your organisation risk averse or adventurous? If it is cash rich, then it might be able to make substantial investments without difficulty. On the other hand, if an organisation is run very lean, then investments might have to be self-financing.

....

The 37th secret of successful Insight teams is that they build a commercial foundation to underpin all their work

If you would like to explore this topic further, you might like to read the IMA's Insight leader guide *IMP802: How to build a commercial foundation for Insight*

....

Key points to consider:

1. To optimise its impact, an Insight team needs a commercial foundation to underpin its work

2. A commercial foundation requires a solid fact-base, so we should start by assembling Core Stats

3. These Core Stats are then used to develop a Business Blueprint that we can enhance as we overlay new insights about trends

4. Demonstrate that you have built a firm commercial foundation by writing an Executive Brief suitable for new directors' induction

5. Our Insight teams should also be encouraged to develop and display a commercial mindset during all their day-to-day activity

In chapter 4 we looked at various techniques that we could use when dealing with imperfect or incomplete data. Some of those techniques are particularly useful when we want to calculate the commercial value inherent in a business issue. This is the topic that we'll explore in the next chapter.

Chapter 38
The value of valuation

A few years ago the Insight forum met in London to discuss the ways in which our departments could optimise their impact. Over 40 Insight leaders took part that day, representing organisations as diverse as Avis Budget Group, Lucozade Ribena Suntory, Intercontinental Hotels Group, Prudential and ANZ Bank. And because we wanted to understand how we could better influence senior directors, we thought it would be a good idea to include a senior decision-maker in the discussion. We were delighted to be joined by Sue Whelan Tracey, at that time a board director at Moneyfacts, as well as a National Health Service trust, a diabetes charity, and the UK's Independent Police Complaints Commission. She had previously run major banking operations in the UK, Caribbean and Africa.

At the end of the session I asked Sue if she thought there was anything else that Insight leaders could do to effect a step change in their teams' impact. Her answer was simple but profound. She said that throughout her career she had been a champion of Customer Insight and always wanted to involve Insight departments in more decisions. But she and her senior colleagues routinely hit a *language* barrier: the Insight team talked the language of *customer* and the rest of the organisation, including all the senior people, talked the language of *finance*.

All major companies, whether in the commercial, charity or public sector, reverberate to the sound of the language of finance. Conversations are dominated by the latest sales figures, or shortfalls in revenue targets, the spiralling costs of operations, or profits and their effect on share prices. Success and failure are denominated in dollars, pounds and euros, and it's financial measures that frame perceptions of every issue being discussed.

So when senior people reach out to Insight for help, they are trying to solve issues which they see through a financial lens, and they will describe the decisions to be made using financial language. And what do we do? Well most Insight teams will diligently research the issues and then report back in the language of *customer*: we talk about brand health measures, customer satisfaction, NPS, Link testing and market share; we reference methodologies like semiotics, ethnography or focus groups, and use jargon like database variables, calculated attributes, confidence scores, maybe even r2 values from our regression models! To others it must seem as if we live in our own world, speaking our own language.

Now you might be reading this and thinking, but surely that's a good thing? Insight teams need to speak the language of the customer, and the world would be a better place if more people in my company adopted our perspective. In some ways, of course, you'd be right, but the reality is that if all the senior decision-makers speak one language today and we speak another, it's no surprise if we struggle to optimise our impact. As Sue Whelan Tracey went on to say at the Insight forum, it is a mistake to put senior executives in a position where *they* have to translate our work into their language 'through the filter of their own ignorance'. In other words, business leaders, understandably, do not have the knowledge necessary to bridge from our language to theirs, so if we want customer insights to be accurately reflected in big decisions we have to translate them into the language that others understand. We can't leave the translation to others.

The value of valuation

Valuation techniques play a critical role in this process. The IMA's founder, Steve Wills, calls them 'the crankshaft of Insight commerciality'. Valuation draws from the bank of internal and external Core Stats I introduced in chapter 37 and converts them into commercial value equivalents. All we need to calculate the size of the prize is:

a) The scope of the area affected by the decision

b) The quantified, desired outcome for the organisation

Let's take a simple example. Say the aim of a business project is to improve customer churn by 10% or 50,000 customers per year. If you know from analysis that each customer is worth roughly £300 in revenue per year, then the potential size of the prize is £15m. This sort of valuation quickly allows you to gauge the relative importance of a business issue as measured in financial – and hence commercial – terms. And it's done using the BOEING technique that we looked at near the start of *Transforming Insight* in chapter 4.

Valuation enables an Insight team to have a clear understanding of the biggest commercial opportunities and threats faced by the organisation and to assess the potential commercial value of any given business issue. This information can then be added to the emerging Business Blueprint and help the Insight team to prioritise their work and provide more commercial insights.

As we saw in chapter 4, it is more important for Insight teams to be broadly right than precisely wrong. The key thing is not to over-complicate our BOEINGs; if we spend more than 10 minutes on them we are probably trying to be too clever.

……

The 38th secret of successful Insight teams is that they use simple valuation techniques to translate their work into the language of finance

If you would like to explore this topic further, you might like to read the IMA's Insight leader guide *IMP803: How to identify commercial value*

……

Key points to consider:

1. Insight teams tend to speak their own language, with its unique phrases, acronyms and three letter abbreviations
2. The rest of our organisations, including senior executives, speak a different language: the language of finance
3. This creates a language barrier that prevents even the most customer-orientated directors from including insights in decisions
4. Senior business leaders are not qualified to translate Insight work into the language of finance; we must do our own translation
5. Simple valuation techniques help us to look at issues through a commercial lens and provide insights the business can understand

Having built a commercial foundation for Insight, and become adept at simple valuation exercises using BOEING, we can now apply our understanding to day-to-day activity. We'll look at some of the most important applications in the next chapter.

Chapter 39
Applying commercial thinking

An Insight team should aim to help its organisation become more commercial by contributing quantified understanding about the financial implications of how and why consumers in its market become customers of that organisation. The first steps are to develop a commercial foundation for all its work and to become adept at simple valuation techniques. These can help us to see customer issues through a financial lens and use the language of finance to make business recommendations.

These measures in themselves can make a significant difference for the organisation, and simultaneously enhance the Insight team's reputation for commercial thinking and optimise its impact. However, to really make an ongoing difference, an Insight team also has to demonstrate a commercial mindset in its everyday activities, applying the understanding it has developed to the way it operates each week.

How can an Insight team apply commercial thinking?

There are three important ways in which our Insight teams can apply their commercial thinking:

- What we do: use value to prioritise our activity
- How we do it: use each piece of work to identify value opportunities

- What we have done: record the value opportunities we have identified and those that have been actioned

What we do

Most Insight teams in the UK, North America and Europe currently prioritise their activity using one of following methods:

- We do what we normally do
- We respond to requests from those who shout loudest
- We rank projects according to the seniority of the person who asked
- We operate on a first come first served basis

These are all sub-optimal for a progressive Insight team. If our underlying purpose is to identify value and drive change, then we need to focus on business issues where we have the potential to add most value. Therefore, one of the most tangible ways of optimising our impact is to re-engineer the process by which we prioritise the work that our teams do.

Valuation techniques should play a key part in the prioritisation process, with a disproportionate focus given to projects that we estimate to have the biggest commercial upside. The good news is that once our teams have become accustomed to valuing projects, we can develop some simple rules of thumb that make the process even easier. A good example of this comes from international brewers, Molson Coors, who were one of the first Insight teams to develop a matrix explaining to their business how the Insight team would adopt a 'full research – light research – no research' approach to requests based on the value of the brand in question and the nature of the business decision to be taken. Based on empirical data, the matrix helped everyone to understand that some decisions (for example a major TV advertising campaign for one of their biggest beer brands like UK market leader Carling) would justify a full research project, whilst a quick repackaging exercise for one of their smallest brands might not justify any new primary research at all.

How we do it

In chapters 5 and 6, I outlined a 7-step process for first nailing and then investigating business issues. At each stage of that journey, corporate Insight professionals can build on their commercial foundations and demonstrate a commercial mindset:

Reflect: Before starting a new project we should always reflect on what we know, and include within that our Core Stats and Business Blueprint.

Engage: before responding to requests we need to speak to decision-makers, probing to understand the commercial context behind their request.

Diagnose: using the SCQAB model to nail the issue and structure our thinking, we include Core Stats in the Situation and Complication sections and link our key Question to the underlying sources of value.

Hypothesis: our initial attempts to scope potential solutions should reference commercial realities and operational constraints.

Explore: our focus will probably turn primarily to discovering relevant customer and market data at this point, but...

Interpret: we must then interpret our customer and market evidence using the context of Core Stats and the Business Blueprint to see if our findings are commercially significant.

Opinions: our recommendations for what the organisation should do now must be based on commercial understanding, with the SCQAB benefits expressed in financial language.

What we have done

Too often there is a tendency to move onto the next project and lose sight of what our colleagues in other departments did with our insights, and this is a real handicap to Insight teams that want to optimise their impact. The best solution is to create a Value Log that records the projects undertaken and the potential opportunities identified, then to arrange follow-up meetings with decision-makers to check what business activity happened as a result and how that affected revenue and costs. This data becomes invaluable for assessing future requests, and the Value Log also becomes critical to another aspect of Insight effectiveness explored in the next chapter.

Commercial role models

Experience has taught us that adopting a commercial mindset and applying it to day-to-day Insight activity requires an ongoing focus and will only succeed if:

- The Insight leader role-models commercial behaviours
- A champion(s) is identified to re-enforce those behaviours

Everything to do with commerciality will initially feel a bit strange to some Insight managers, researchers and analysts, and it is common for an initial bout of enthusiasm to be followed by a slide back into old habits. Value Logs become neglected, prioritisation of work reverts to how it was done before, and the Insight team misses out on a golden opportunity to optimise its impact. But a determined, visible leader, assisted by an enthusiastic team champion, can make all the difference.

....

The 39th secret of successful Insight teams is that they demonstrate commerciality as they prioritise, execute and record their work

If you would like to explore this topic further, you might like to read the IMA's Insight leader guide *IMP804: How to apply commercial thinking in Insight*

....

Key points to consider:

1. Having built a commercial foundation, an Insight team has to demonstrate a commercial mindset in its everyday activities
2. It should prioritise its work based on the relative value of the various projects that it could undertake at any moment in time
3. It should demonstrate commerciality as it executes each project, spotting value opportunities whenever it can
4. It should record the value opportunities that it identifies and track what the organisation does in response to its recommendations
5. To continuously progress, Insight teams need their leaders and commercial champions to role-model commercial behaviour

In this chapter we've explored a range of ways in which Insight teams can demonstrate a commercial perspective to all their work. But to truly optimise our impact, we need to go one step further and calculate the Insight return on investment. That's what we'll look at in the next chapter.

Chapter 40
Investing in Insight

Putting a value to Insight has been seen as a kind of Holy Grail for the market research and Insight industry for a long time. However, the predominant view has usually been that it can't really be done because Insight is simply part of a value chain, our work being one small part of a larger picture.

But is this really true? Let's consider a simplified business process like new product development to see if the argument holds water:

- Initial idea
- Research and development
- Produce product
- Market the product
- Sell it and make money

In new product development a value can be placed on the overall process and the money it makes. But many people would argue that to place a value on any single element is not really possible, because anyone in the chain could claim that if they hadn't done their bit then the business would have made no money. We need the initial idea, and the production, and the selling to make any money at all.

This argument makes sense for all the elements that are really essential, but it doesn't apply to elements that are discretionary. Steve Wills uses car manufacture as an example. Many of the parts assembled to make our cars are essential to our ability to drive them - you cannot have a car at all without wheels, seats and a steering wheel – and that makes it impossible to put a value on those individual elements. However, a lot of money spent on cars relates to parts that are not essential to their basic function – like the material used on the seats and steering wheel, the cup holders, entertainment systems, sunroofs, etc. These elements are discretionary, and that means that the automotive industry can give us a choice about which we have and don't have, and also charge us extra for them.

So you cannot put an individual value on the essential elements in a process, but you can put a value on those that are discretionary.

Is Insight essential or discretionary?

It might seem very odd for a book dedicated to making Insight teams more effective to argue that what we do is actually discretionary. But when you stop and think about it, there are plenty of companies out there making decisions every day in a way that could be described as 'Insight-free'. Either there is no customer and market Insight involved at all, or it is introduced too late to make much of a difference, or the quality of the research or analysis is sub-optimal. The company that you work for probably has an Insight team, but consider all the decisions that it currently takes about new products, marketing, store closures, pricing, customer propositions and corporate strategy: do you consider all these decisions to be completely and consistently Insight-driven?

The reality is that our organisations will make hundreds of decisions every year that are Insight-free not Insight-driven. They may not be very good decisions, but they are made anyway! This is the very essence of why we need to make our Insight teams more effective and why we should all learn from those that are. But it also demonstrates that the use of insights is discretionary, and like any part of a value chain that is discretionary, that means we can estimate the incremental value of including it.

The Insight valuation process

The good news is that if our Insight teams are already completing the Value Logs described in the last chapter, they will already have most of the components they need to calculate the value of Insight:

- The scale of the overall issue
- The size of the prize associated with the specific business decision
- The value opportunities identified by the Insight team
- The actual benefits realised by the organisation

All we need to complete our calculation is the percentage of the benefits realised that can be assigned to the input from the Insight team, and then a comparison with how much that Insight involvement really cost - the third party research spend, data purchase, staff time, even database and infrastructure costs if you want to be really comprehensive.

What proportion of success is down to Insight?

The sticking point for many Insight teams is that they think they can't value their own input. But there are two bits of even better news here.

First, aim for accuracy not precision: in chapter 4, I said that Insight teams should always value accuracy over precision, and this applies to our commercial valuation work, including the value we put on our own contribution. If you work through a few examples of the initiatives you have influenced, you will quickly discover that a successful business outcome is likely to be worth so much more to your organisation than the cost of your involvement, that the precise % assigned to Insight's contribution is immaterial.

For example, let's suppose that one of the IMA's members like Carlsberg or Kraft-Heinz brings out a new product that adds £25m to revenue (a drop in the ocean to companies of their size) and the Insight team spent £125k on research and analysis. If we estimated the value of the Insight contribution at 5% of the £25m (£1.25m) that would equate to a 10-fold return on the £125k spent on Insight. If you valued Insight's contribution at 10% of the £25m, that would give you a 20-fold return (£2.5m divided by £125k). These ROI figures are so high that even if you always took the lower of two estimates, the benefit of including Insight is plain. What matters is not whether we contribute 5% or 10%, it's that we work on very large, successful business initiatives.

Second, we don't even need to estimate the value of our own contribution; other departments can do that for us. eBay were one of the first IMA members to routinely ask colleagues in other departments to estimate their perception of Insight's contribution. What surprised the Insight team was that their colleagues in Marketing and Sales consistently valued the Insight contribution more highly than the Insight team did themselves. It wasn't unusual for the other departments to say that 25% or 30% of the value uplift was down to Insight, whereas the Insight team themselves were cautious about claiming more than 20%. Barclays Insight team has seen the same phenomenon; their Head of UK Insight has a policy of not claiming more than 20% of the benefit of any initiative even if feedback from the business suggests that it was probably higher.

The key takeout here is that the return on an organisation's investment in Insight is likely to be extremely high, but only if the team focuses its efforts on the biggest business issues. And that return will only be evident to anyone if the Insight team itself starts to record the numbers and calculate the uplift. Of course, we need input from colleagues in other departments, but even if we only valued a proportion of our projects, it is likely that we would be seen to have paid back our organisation many times its investment in Insight. And that's always going to be a useful thing to know if we find ourselves defending our resources or arguing for an expansion in Insight activity.

......

The 40th secret of successful Insight teams is that they calculate their organisation's return on its investment in Insight

If you would like to explore this topic further, you might like to read the IMA's Insight leader guide *IMP805: An introduction to Insight return on investment*

......

Key points to consider:

1. Calculating a return on investment for Insight has long been seen as a Holy Grail, often assumed to be impossible
2. The IMA believes that it is possible to estimate an Insight ROI because in reality the use of Insight is always discretionary
3. Insight teams should already know the size of the initiatives, the value opportunities they spot, and the value actually realised
4. They then estimate the proportion of the value that can be assigned to Insight and compare this to the time and budget spent
5. Organisations can generate millions in revenue by spending thousands on Insight and estimating ROI helps to support Insight expansion

This chapter completes section 4, and our focus on *Optimising Impact.* However, there are two further secrets to share, both of them connected with the theme of *Moving Forwards.*

Section 5

Moving forwards

Moving forwards

In this final section of *Transforming Insight*, we will focus on the last two secrets of successful corporate Insight teams:

Chapter 41
Accelerating the evolution of Insight

In the introduction to *Transforming Insight* I said that this was the best time ever to work in a corporate Insight team. A combination of better data, enhanced understanding of consumer psychology, and an increasing appetite from senior management has presented Insight teams with a greater opportunity than ever before. It's a message I have repeated many times over the last three years, but I didn't have the opportunity to write a book about it until 2020 when the coronavirus pandemic led to global lockdown and a change in all our working patterns.

For the first forty chapters I have hardly mentioned the coronavirus, because the secrets I have shared are based on best practice principles discussed over two decades. It is always unwise to make hasty decisions about how deep principles can be applied to fast-moving circumstances when it is far from clear how long the new circumstances will last or the ripple effect they will have on our societies, our economies and the organisations for which we work. But some months on, as shops re-open their doors and more and more people return to work, it would also be wrong not to reflect on the conversations held with IMA members during the lockdown and share some early observations.

The first thing to say is that Insight has now been propelled into the limelight as never before. When I normally talk to progressive Insight leaders about the need for their departments to 'map from the market to the money' they immediately get the idea, but the detail can sometimes seem rather conceptual to their colleagues. The bigger the company we work for, the more isolated we often become from the commercial reality on which our organisation is founded. We work with Sales, Marketing, Product, Channel, Finance and Strategy teams who are themselves stove-piped, obsessing over their own day-to-day busyness which often masks our fundamental reliance on consumers continuing to become customers and create value for us through their interactions.

But the commercial bones of our organisations have been laid bare by the pandemic. When every news headline declares that another company will bite the dust, it is impossible for us not to consider how the current environment is shaping consumer choices, and how customer behaviour has a very tangible effect on our commercial success. If your colleagues ever doubted that the market *Environment* framed consumer *Decisions* which drove customer *Activity* and impacted organisational *Metrics*, they're not going to doubt it now.

Whether your company has only just survived or positively thrived over the last few months, the *MADE in Insight* model will provide you with a lens for showing how your situation is similar or different to other companies. With members drawn from every industry segment - public sector, education and charity as well as commercial - the IMA has spoken to Insight leaders whose organisations have traded well above expectations in 2020 as well as those who have really struggled. But whatever the impact so far, the key take-out is the same: all our organisations need Insight more than ever before, and it is going to be a very brave - and foolish – CEO who makes decisions in the next few months about re-opening, re-launching, re-stucturing or re-positioning their company without consulting the Insight team.

In response to this exposure, our Insight teams are frantically adjusting to the circumstances within which they now operate. The biggest problem for them is that the market research techniques on which they normally rely, and the data sources from which they draw metrics, have both been devised under very different circumstances. Moreover, consumers themselves simply don't know how they are going to behave in a few months' time because they don't know the options that will be available to them or the circumstances in which they will be making their decisions. In some respects, this is less of a change than it first appears because we are all poor analysts of our own behaviour at the best of times and as consumers we frequently do things driven by reasons we cannot fathom. But if consumers can't tell you what they will do next under normal conditions, they have no chance now.

Therefore, the most effective Insight teams are instead doing what we should have been doing all along. They are focusing on finding new and multiple sources of data from which they can develop a joined-up understanding of the possible scenarios. They are editing the plethora of information bombarding our companies, evaluating the credibility of new evidence, forming an opinion about the possible courses of action, and communicating it to senior stakeholders in very clear, succinct digests. They are focusing ruthlessly on the issues that could have a profound commercial effect and using their own Core Stats and Business Blueprints to calculate possible commercial outcomes. Far from moving away from the principles explored in this book, they are embracing them more enthusiastically. They are identifying value through new insights and customer knowledge, driving change through influence and communication, leading Insight strategy and people, and optimising the impact of Insight for the benefit of their organisations.

It has probably become apparent to you already, but now is the time to accelerate the evolution of Insight. The pandemic has presented us with an unprecedented opportunity to stop old habits and create new ones based on best practice principles. If we act now, we can reposition our Insight teams for the future. Even more importantly, we can transform the effectiveness of our Insight teams at a moment when our organisations need Insight like never before.

......

The 41st secret of successful Insight teams is that they seize every opportunity to position Insight for success in the future

If you would like to reflect on this topic further, please feel free to explore the latest thinking on the IMA website, www.insight-management.org

......

Key points to consider:

1. There has never been a greater time to work in a corporate Insight team, nor a bigger opportunity for Insight to make a difference
2. The coronavirus pandemic has made it extremely difficult for any responsible CEO to make decisions without referring to Insight
3. Existing sources and trusted techniques may prove more difficult to use for some time, and consumers won't know the answers themselves
4. Insight leaders who consult the key principles outlined in this book will stand a far better chance of repositioning Insight for the future
5. This is the time to seize the moment and accelerate the evolution of our Insight departments; our companies' success depends on it

Whether you are reading this whilst your country is still in lockdown, returning to work, or getting back to some form of normality, we can't see the transformation of Insight as a quick win or a one-off exercise. It requires fresh thinking, new ideas, invigorating conversations and dedicated discipline to make Insight make a difference. Therefore, in the final chapter, we will explore ways in which we can all maintain our momentum.

Chapter 42
Maintaining our momentum

After presenting at the Quirk's Event in Brooklyn in March 2019 I flew back to the UK and received a call the next day from the Head of Learning and Development at one of the world's largest FMCG organisations. She said that she'd heard me speak about Insight transformation, and she wanted to know which companies I thought were the furthest ahead when it came to developing their Insight capability and using it to drive corporate performance. Which brands were based on the best insights? Which sector had the most established Insight processes? Which were the world's best Insight-driven organisations?

Feeling rather jet-lagged after the flight back from New York, I walked round and round the garden at the Institute of Directors in central London while I spoke to her, trying to clear my head and frame a sensible answer. I was actually quite surprised at her questions, because the truth was that her company was one of the five global providers who are mentioned most frequently as exemplars of Insight best practice at conferences and in publications like the Harvard Business Review. At the end of my description of how Insight capability could be developed and used to drive decisions, there was a long pause, then she said: 'Wow, I wish it was like that in my company! We are so far behind with this.'

The point of my story is that there are very few truly Insight-driven organisations in the world, and even those Insight teams that are famous within the research and analysis community may not be seen as exemplars within their own organisation. In fact there are times when I'd almost say that the inverse is true: many of the Insight leaders whom I most respect would tell you that they have a very long way to go before they have transformed their Insight team and the role it plays in their business. It is not just what they have achieved that I admire, it is their willingness to accept new ideas, to be impressed by work done in far smaller organisations, and their determination to press on with their mission to make Insight make more of a difference this year than it did last year.

So, now that you have read the first 41 chapters of this book, I'm going to repeat the question that I asked you right at the very start:

Do you work for an Insight-driven organisation?

If the answer is yes, then I'm delighted that your company has recognised the potential for customer and market insights to drive big decisions, and that the Insight function itself has developed the capability to fulfil its potential.

But if you feel that your Insight team is not yet the best it could be, maybe even that it's somewhere behind where it should be or where you imagine it to be in other organisations, my message would be: don't worry, you are really not alone.

Having spoken to hundreds of Insight leaders over the last two decades and benchmarked over 200 organisations during the last couple of years, the Insight Management Academy's view is that very few Insight teams have attained the highest level of performance across many of the principles described in this book. Don't get me wrong, there are some brilliant insights being generated, some fantastic work done to build knowledge, some communication ideas adopted that are so many times better than anything I'd have ever thought of. But there is no single organisation that comes top of the IMA's benchmarking on all measures. There is always something new for everyone to learn.

So if you recognise that you need to transform your Insight team and the role it plays in your organisation, I'd like to reassure you that the 42nd secret of successful Insight teams is that they always know they can do better, but they find ways to maintain their momentum, even when it feels like circumstances are against them. I know it's a corny thing to say, but all Insight teams are on a journey, so let me suggest five simple steps to help you to move forwards on yours.

Step 1: read widely and expose yourself to new ideas: You have actually just completed Step 1, or at least shown your willingness to embrace it! There are not many books out there dedicated to transforming corporate Insight teams, but there are some great articles, blogs and conference presentations. There are also books written about different subjects but from which progressive Insight leaders have much to learn. I've listed some personal favourites in the Further Reading section that follows this chapter.

Step 2: consider the current state of Insight in your company: Find ways to talk to senior decision-makers in your company and discuss your ideas with them. Feel free to share any of the principles we've explored in *Transforming Insight*, but don't expect universal acceptance of them. Without knowing an Insight team from the inside it is very difficult to understand the potential that Insight could make, and even more difficult to get your head around the steps you'd need to take to realise that potential. So it's best to talk about outcomes: how could your organisation improve its performance if your department played a different role?

Step 3: review the effectiveness of your Insight team: If you have enjoyed the *42 secrets* shared here, the IMA has a free benchmarking tool, the *Transforming Insight* survey (see www.insight-management.org), that we can make available to any corporate Insight leader. It uses the same framework as the *Transforming Insight* book, and we will send you a report showing how your responses compare to a benchmark constructed from all the other responses.

Step 4: reflect on your priorities: Even if your Insight team has already embraced many of the best practice principles in this book, it will still take some time to work on all the rest. We all need to work out the priority areas to work on in each period. If you have the chance to write an Insight strategy, that is always going to be a good place to start. But developing and executing a strategy will itself take some time, so you will probably want to address areas like Insight generation, knowledge farming, communication or influence in parallel. If your Insight team is not really connected to the rest of your organisation, it might be best to start with commerciality. Or if your researchers and analysts do the basics well but never get any credit for it, you could start with positioning. If you want to take the *Transforming Insight* survey, the results will offer plenty of suggestions.

Step 5: reach out to other Insight leaders: There are some excellent membership organisations in the UK, North America, Europe and Asia, all offering networking opportunities, and some offering advice. If you want to learn more about the technical aspects of market research it is best to approach one of the large research organisations like ESOMAR, the global market research organisation, or AURA in the UK whose members get to showcase the Insight projects they have developed with research agencies. You can also see great case studies at Insight conferences, with Quirk's for one providing fabulous events in New York, Chicago and London. The IMA itself runs the Insight forums for organisations that want to take Insight transformation seriously, and we also provide a range of corporate memberships which offer online learning, advice and flexible support.

However you choose to do it, reach out to other Insight leaders. It can be a surprisingly lonely job if you are the senior Insight professional in a large organisation, with relatively little chance that anyone else in your company will have performed your role or have particular insights into how to do it effectively. But the IMA was founded on the principle of corporate Insight leaders having conversations to discuss best practice, and it's a principle that has helped the IMA in turn to inspire, support and guide several thousand Insight professionals who have felt motivated to transform their Insight teams.

......

The 42nd secret of successful Insight teams is that they review, reflect and reset to maintain their momentum

If you have the ambition to transform your Insight team, the IMA provides inspiration, support and guidance to corporate members

......

Key points to consider:

1. If you have read this book, you have already taken the first step to transform your Insight team!

2. The second step is to consider the current state of Insight in your company: do you already work for an Insight-driven organisation?

3. The third step is to review the effectiveness of your Insight team; you can complete the *Transforming Insight* survey for free at www.insight-management.org

4. The fourth step is to reflect on your priorities: we cannot change everything at once, we need a proper plan

5. The fifth step is to reach out to others who have experience in corporate Insight; there are times we all need support

This concludes our exploration of the 42 secrets of successful corporate Insight teams. If it has inspired you to transform the Insight function in your organisation then I'd like to wish you the very best of luck and offer the IMA's support and guidance whenever you feel you need it.

Also published by the IMA

If you would like to read more, the IMA has published a range of online Insight leader guides for its members:

IMP001: An introduction to successful Insight management

IMP101: An introduction to successful Insight generation

IMP102: How to create joined-up insight

IMP103: How to make up the numbers

IMP104: How to nail the business issue

IMP105: How to approach Insight investigations

IMP201: An introduction to farming Insight knowledge

IMP202: How to sow the seeds of Insight knowledge (coming soon)

IMP203: How to cultivate customer knowledge (coming soon)

IMP204: How to adopt knowledge systems (coming soon)

IMP301: An introduction to influencing decision-makers

IMP302: How to understand decision-makers

IMP303: How to improve stakeholder relationships

IMP304: Influencing skills for introverts

IMP305: Behavioural economics for Insight teams

IMP306: How to nudge decision-makers

IMP401: An introduction to successful Insight communication

IMP402: How to plan an Insight communication programme

IMP403: How to structure Insight communications

IMP404: Storytelling for Insight teams

Also available

IMP405: Visual communication for Insight teams

IMP501: An introduction to Insight strategy

IMP502: How to identify the opportunity for Insight

IMP503: How to define your ambition for Insight

IMP504: How to identify options for your Insight team

IMP505: How to execute an Insight strategy

IMP601: An introduction to developing successful Insight people

IMP602: How to lead an Insight team

IMP603: How to identify key Insight skills and attributes

IMP604: How to develop an Insight perspective

IMP605: How to recruit and develop and Insight team

IMP606: How to develop successful Insight teamwork

IMP701: An introduction to successful Insight positioning

IMP702: How to develop the Insight team brand

IMP703: How to promote awareness of Insight

IMP704: How to improve your Insight team's reputation

IMP705: How to improve Insight's role in key processes

IMP801: An introduction to Insight commerciality

IMP802: How to build a commercial foundation for Insight

IMP803: How to identify commercial value

IMP804: How to apply commercial thinking in Insight

IMP805: An introduction to Insight return on investment

Further reading

There are very few books written for corporate Insight professionals, but there are many books out there from which we can learn. The following is a selection of those from which my colleagues and I have drawn ideas and inspiration when developing the principles described in this book:

Collins, Jim (2001). *Good to Great*

Covey, Stephen R. (2004 revised edition). *The 7 Habits of Highly Effective People*

Duncan, Kevin (2013). *The Diagrams Book*

Eastaway, Rob (2019). *Maths on the Back of an Envelope*

Gerber, Michael (2001). *The E-Myth Revisited*

Halpern, David (2015). *Inside the Nudge Unit*

Heath, Chip and Dan (2008). *Made to Stick*

Kahneman, Daniel (2011). *Thinking, Fast and Slow*

Maister, D., Green, C. and Galford, R. (2000). *The Trusted Advisor*

McCandless, David (2009). *Information is Beautiful*

Minto, Barbara (1987). *The Pyramid Principle*

Ridley, Matt (2020). *How Innovation Works*

Rosling, Hans (2018). *Factfulness*

Sharp, Byron (2010). *How Brands Grow*

Shotton, Richard (2018). *The Choice Factory*

Sutherland, Rory (2019). *Alchemy*

Syed, Matthew (2015). *Black Box Thinking*

Thaler, Richard H. and Sunstein, Cass R. (2009). *Nudge*

Acknowledging my colleagues

The IMA is a very collegiate organisation where we constantly develop ideas by discussing experiences and sharing opinions. I'd like to acknowledge the enormous contribution that my colleagues at the IMA have made to every page of this book, with special thanks to:

Tim Downing, for chapters 6, 32, 39

Lisa Dutton, for chapters 6, 13, 19

Juliet Jessop, for chapter 12

Emma Jones, for chapters 10, 35

Julia Joskey, for chapters 4, 14, 20, 33

Sally Webb, for chapters 1, 5, 16, 18

Steve Wills, for chapters 1, 13, 15, 36, 38, 40

Jane Woolley, for chapters 6, 25, 28, 30, 34

Acknowledging our members

I would like to thank all the IMA members and other organisations whose Insight leaders have contributed to our thinking over the last year, including:

Abcam
Abellio
Alexion Pharma
Allianz
Asda
Audible
Aviva
Barclays Bank
Barnet Waddingham LLP
Boehringer Ingelheim
British Gas
British Heart Foundation
Carlsberg
Capital One
Carnival
Central England Co-op
Co-operative Group
Coventry Building Society
DFS Group
Dignity Funeralcare
Dixons Carphone
Dow Jones
Dublin Airports Authority
Dyson
eBay
Futures Housing Group
Gamesys
GlaxoSmithKline
Gymshark
Highways England
HM Land Registry
HM Revenue & Customs
John Lewis Partnership
Kraft-Heinz
Legal & General
Leonard Cheshire Disability
Lloyd's Register
Lloyds Banking Group
Lucozade Ribena Suntory
Marks & Spencer
Marston's
McDonald's
N. Brown
National Public Radio of America
Nationwide Building Society
NEC Group
Nestle
News UK
NFU Mutual
Northumbrian Water
Novozymes
Oxford University Press
Premier Foods
Primark
RBS
Royal Mail
Sainsbury's
Santander
Simply Health
Skipton Building Society
Sofology
Spire Healthcare
Sport England
Sport Wales
Spotify
SSE
St James's Place
Suunto
Talk Talk
Tesco
The Open University
TI Media
Transport for Greater Manchester
Transport for London
Twinings
University of Manchester
Virgin Media
Waitrose
Warburtons
Westpac
Western Union
Which?
Whitbread
Wilko
Yodel